CHRISTMAS 2025 with Love

I bet you cook something! out of here, you're such a
good chef. I found this in a thrift & saw the author lives on co
from MB. The "rock" "our rock at the ocean" on the cover. Wow is what your mom said.

GARDENS-BY-THE-BAY
COOKBOOK

GARDENS-BY-THE-BAY

COOKBOOK

Herbs & Natural Gourmet Foods Cooking

Lisa Curtis

1993

SAND RIVER PRESS

LOS OSOS, CALIFORNIA

Copies of this book may be obtained by sending $10.95 + 1.50 postage and handling to: SAND RIVER PRESS, 1319 14th St. LOS OSOS, CA. 93402.
CALIFORNIA residents please add appropriate sales tax.
Printed in the United States of America.

Designed by Bruce W. Miller
Cover art and interior illustrations John Landon

ISBN 0-944627-37-4

DEDICATION

This book is dedicated to my mother, the most inspired and creative cook I will ever
know!

...to the memories of Aida and Hanna, two best old friends
who loved everything I ever cooked.

ACKNOWLEDGEMENTS

...First and foremost, to my dear friend and the original designer of this project, Diana Bistagne! This is a woman with an innate ability to turn chaos into order and since my middle name is Chaos, we make a great team! It is only through Diana's inspiration, support and creative energy that I hung in there long enough to see this book through. Through her business, Design, Etc., Diana shares her skills with those lucky enough to find her!

...To Bruce Miller for picking up the project when I had given up.

...To all my friends, The Tasters, who not only listened to me jabber about this book for two years, but who willingly and bravely sampled my recipes—over and over again! Especially thanks to Bob (my husband) who never complained and who supported me in every way possible.

...To all recipe contributors. MANY thanks for offering such variety and color to the project.

...Last, but certainly not least, to my mother, Barbara, who contributed so many recipes and so much invaluable advice on all aspects of cooking.

THE FOLLOWING PEOPLE HAVE CONTRIBUTED INVALUABLE IDEAS AND/ OR RECIPES TO THIS PROJECT...MANY THANKS TO ALL!

Bob Matchett (#1 Taster and Critic)
Barbara Coker (Thank you, mother!)
Melinda Forbes (my herb mentor!)
Lindee Cox, Janet Storey, Julie P. Block, Jean Ogden, Diana Bistagne,
Betty Davidson, Connie Keeney, Nancy Walker, Mark Goddard

INTRODUCTION

Gardens By The Bay Cookbook is more than another treatise
on health food or cooking with herbs, although its varied themes
include both. It is strongly influenced by vegetarianism and by
regional, ethnic foods. Most of all, the recipes are geared for ease
of cooking, short preparation times and a spirit of creativity in the
kitchen. As you use this book you will gain an appreciation for fresh,
quality ingredients and for the ability to choose prepared foods of
high quality when time limitations require it. The best cooks are
those who "taste as they go," change a recipe to suit their desires
without fear of experimentation, and most of all those who have a
lot of fun preparing the foods they love to eat. The recipes in this
book are designed with these factors in mind, They are presented
in a format that allows substitutions for varied tastes and that allows
the cook to be flexible enough to take advantage of the best seasonal
foods, always with wonderful results!

The Gardens By The Bay Cookbook is an outgrowth of my
company of the same name. I produce a line of herbal gourmet
foods and grow fresh herbs. When I started selling herbal vinegars,
herbed oils and salads dressings, people asked for sample recipes in
which to use them. I started looking through recipes to choose a few
for a small booklet to include with the products and realized that I

had more than a few. I had many notebooks and files, full of great recipes that I had collected over the years from family and friends, through extensive travel and through many experiments with herbs in developing my products. A cookbook seemed the prefect way to organize the recipes and share them at the same time.

I was raised on Tex-Mex Soul Food. The diet was full of wonderful flavors and, unfortunately, full of meat. As a young adult I became a vegetarian and went through a period of macrobiotic experimentation. I found the diet too restrictive for the long haul but there were elements that I loved and kept as I developed my own style of cooking. Though I have come a long way from the days when the best seasoning was a ham hock or a slab of bacon fat, I have also come a long way from the days when I tested my food with litmus paper and drank burdock root tea instead of coffee! The result is a varied vegetarian diet, full of the best flavors and ingredients from both worlds. Herbs have replaced the meats for seasonings, along with foods like tofu and rice and beans for the protein; but corn, hot chiles, greens and lentils remain. The diets developed my taste for spicy, varied ethnic foods of all kinds. In my travels to Mexico, the Bahamas, the West Indies, and Europe, I picked up a wonderful collection of regional dishes and adapted them to a vegetarian palate. A friend owned a Chinese restaurant in Santa Cruz a "few" (as I get older, it's hard to admit just how many) years ago and her best loved dishes appear here as a first. I had the privilege of growing up best friends with a family of great Italian cooks whose best secrets also appear here as a first. So you are in for a wonderful epicurean adventure!

Vegetarianism will do your heart good in more ways than one. I "converted" twenty-one years ago purely for ethical reasons. The result has been an incredible growth in my interest in good food, rather than the restriction you might expect. Another wonderful result has been good health. All of the recipes in this book are vegetarian, and all are healthy compared to a diet which includes meat. But, regardless of your dietary preference, these foods will appeal to your tastebuds! Concensus among meat-eaters seems to be that vegetarian foods are bland...not so, as you will discover!

The best way to use this book is to open your mind and your tastebuds to a new experience and let the adventure begin...

Enjoy!

TABLE OF CONTENTS

SALADS

Avocado Papaya Salad / 29
Tico's Favorite Primate Salad / 30
North African Carrot Salad / 31
Onion Chive Tofu Salad with Seaweed & Wasabe / 32
Orange Spinach & Basil Salad with Hot Garlic Dressing / 33
Salade Pomme de Terre / 34
Smorgasbord of Dressings:
...Herbed Yogurt / 35
...Lemon-Dill Mayonaise / 35
...Creamy Taragon / 36
...Herbal Vinaigrette with Sun Dried Tomatoes / 36
...Lime Vinaigrette / 37
Angel Hair Pasta with Fresh Tomatoes and Basil / 38
Plain & Pesto Croutons / 39

SOUPS

Miso Soup / 43
Cuban Black Bean Soup / 44
Sherried Carrot and Parsley Soup / 45
Avocado Soup with Sage Cilantro Sauce / 46
Potato Leek Dill Soup / 47
Ice Berg Soup / 48
Ice Berg Tomato Salad / 49
Curried Soup Sandwich / 49
Ice Berg Dip / 49
Soup of Greens / 50

MAIN DISHES

Melinda's Classic Veggie Burgers / 53
Orange Cream Pasta with Spring Flowers / 54
Speedy Spicy Spinach Casserole / 56
Linguini with Fresh Herb Medley Sauce / 57
Chinese Herb Pasta / 58
Spicy Tofu with Hot Peanut Cilantro Sauce / 59
Flowering Chive Stuffed Peppers / 60
Twice Baked Dill Potatoes / 61
Mushroom Herb Loaf / 62
  (The "I'm -afraid- to -call- it -Lentil -Loaf- or -no-one -will-try- it" Loaf!)
Purple Quesadillas / 63
Ginger Asparagus Stir Fry with Cous Cous / 64
Pan Picante / 65
Curried Carrots / 66
Pronto Chili Mole / 67
Easy Cheezy Tacos with Fresh Salsa / 68-69
Chile Relleno Casserole with Guacamole / 70

Special Chinese Dishes
Vegetable Chop Suey / 73
Snow Pea Chop Suey / 74
Tofu Chop Suey / 74
A Side of Tofu / 74
Tofu & Mixed Vegetable Chop Suey / 75
Almon Diced Vegetables / 76
Cashew Tofu / 76
Honey Sweet & Sour Sauce / 77
Sweet & Sour Vegetables / 78
Sweet & Sour Tofu / 78

Tahini Sauce / 79
Cauliflower, Broccoli & Mushrooms in Tahini / 80
Broccoli, Mushrooms & Cabbage in Tahini / 80
Summer Tahini Vegetables / 80
Chop Suey Trilogy:
1. Fresh Water Chestnuts / 81
2. Black Mushrooms / 81
3. Summer Squash / 81
Kung Pao Vegetables / 82

Special Italian Dishes

Tomato Basil Sauce / 85
Ricotta Mushroom Sauce / 85
Lasagna Roll Ups / 86
La Famiglia Marinara / 87
Stuffed Basil Shells / 88
Spinach Basil Tofu Lasagna / 89
Rosemary Foccacia Tortas / 90
Pepper Herb Polenta / 91
Pasta Verano / 93
Broccoli Rissoto / 94

DESSERTS

Kiwi Pear Pie / 97
Mamie B's Red Cake / 98
Rosehips Rice Pudding / 99
Brandied Carob-Mint Bananas with Honeysuckle Vanilla Ice Cream / 100
Ricotta Cheesecake with Melba Sauce / 101-102
Fresh Berry Trifle / 103
Almond Cookie Cafe Almond Cookies / 104
Bergamot Brownies / 105

BREAKFAST

Breakfast has never been one of my favorite meals, primarily because it is eaten in the morning which is not my time of day! Here are some breakfast treats that make it enjoyable, even for the most devoted night person.

WORLD'S BEST HOME FRIES

While traveling through France during the 1970's, I was continually amazed at the delicious treatment of potatoes served at breakfast, as salad at lunch and even as hot salad for dinner. (I was also thrilled at their low cost which is why I sampled them so often!) In experimenting with them at home to try to duplicate the delightful flavor I discovered an herb blend called "Herbes de Provence" which was definitely the key to flavors I had been searching for. This dry herb blend is a delicate combination of traditional culinary herbs used in French and often in other ethnic styles of cooking. It can be purchased pre-blended or to make your own, mix together 1/4 teaspoon each of the following dried herbs: parsley, onion chives, tarragon, chervil, thyme and basil. If using fresh herbs, use 1 teaspoon each, finely chopped. Place the herbs in a clean, dry jar and shake well to blend.

Ingredients

6 large new potatoes (red skinned)
4 tablespoons olive oil
2 tablespoons soy sauce
1 large bell pepper
1/2 teaspoon celery seed.
1/2 teaspoon *Herbes de Provence*
1/4 teaspoon poppy seed.
Dash of red wine to taste
1/4 cup chopped onion—*optional* *
1/2 cup chopped mushrooms—*optional*
2 fresh diced Jalapeños—*optional*

*Onions will add sweetness to the mixture; mushrooms will add flavor and texture as well as volume. The Jalapeños will give it a very hot spike for a Mexican brunch.

Cook potatoes—*steam, boil or microwave,* until tender. Leave the skin on! In a large cast iron skillet on medium high heat place the oil, soy sauce and tobasco. Cook until it begins to bubble. Add the new potatoes and the onions if you choose to use them. Stir until the potatoes are well coated with the oil mixture. Sprinkle the seeds over the potatoes. Reduce heat to medium. Cut the bell pepper into bite-size pieces and add to skillet. Add optional mushrooms now. Let mixture cook for a few minutes and taste it. You may now choose to add additional oil, soy sauce or tobasco according to your taste and to prevent sticking to the pan. Add the dash of red wine to taste. Continue to cook the mixture, stirring occasionally until the potatoes are very tender and begin to get crispy around the edges. I like these potatoes very well done so I cook them for about 15 to 20 minutes.
Serves 4

CINNAMON-OAT CAKES

The batter for these deliciously different pancakes needs to be started the night before but its very easy and well worth it! They are wonderful served with Grilled Grapefruit (pg. 5). Garnish pancakes with pureed fruit, yogurt, a favorite jam or real maple syrup. Skip the butter, you won't miss it.

Ingredients

2 cups regular rolled oats
2 cups buttermilk
2 eggs lightly beaten
1/4 cup margarine melted and cooled
1/2 cup raisins or chopped dates
1/2 cup all-purpose flour
2 tablespoons brown sugar
1 teaspoon baking soda
1/2 teaspoon ground cinnamon
2 teaspoons vanilla extract.

Before bedtime, combine oats and buttermilk in a large bowl, stir to blend and refrigerate. Just before cooking the next morning add eggs, margarine and raisins and stir just enough to blend. In another bowl, stir together flour, sugar, baking powder, soda and cinnamon—add to oats and stir only until moistened. Stir in vanilla. If batter seems too thick, add up to 3 tablespoons more buttermilk.

Preheat griddle or large frying pan over medium heat, grease lightly. Spoon batter (about 1/3 cup at a time) onto griddle in 4 inch circles. Cook until tops are bubbly and dry. Turn and cook other side until lightly browned. Heat plates in oven while you are cooking pancakes so that when they are served they will stay hot longer and everyone can eat together!

Recipe makes about eighteen pancakes.

GRILLED ORANGE-MINT GRAPEFRUIT

Orange-mint, or Bergamot, grows as thick as a forest all through my garden in the spring and summer. It is a most delightfully scented plant which I use to add delicate flavor to many dishes including this outrageous breakfast grapefruit. Serve as a light meal with toast or as the first course in a full brunch. The addition of this colorful herb turns ordinary grapefruit into a work of art.

Ingredients:

Large ruby-pink grapefruit (1/2 per person)
1/2 teaspoon honey for each grapefruit half
1 teaspoon Grande Marnier/ half
1 sprig fresh Bergamot/half (pick a sprig with at least 3 nice leaves)
Bergamot flowers (for garnish) if available

Slice grapefruit in half and section with a grapefruit knife. Discard seeds when possible without destroying the sections of fruit. Place one sprig of orange-mint, stem down, in the center of each grapefruit half and spread leaves evenly onto the fruit to make it visually pleasing. Drizzle the Grande Marnier over each half, followed by the honey. Place grapefruit halves on a flat pan and grill under broiler just until they begin to brown slightly (watch carefully, they will burn easily). When piping hot and bubbling (about 5 min.), remove and serve immediately. Garnish plates with flowers if you have them (use other seasonal flowers if Bergamot is not yet blooming).

HUEVOS TAVOS BREAKFAST BURRITOS

*This delightfully quick breakfast is filling and healthy, combining the wonderful flavors of cilantro and Mexican oregano to bring out the best in eggs (or tofu, as you choose). My good friend, Lola, the best cook in Santiago, Colima (Mexico) makes this dish in a large cast iron skillet, over an open-air stove. She has the advantage of picking the chiles, oregano and cilantro fresh from the garden she planted around her "kitchen". Try growing your own herbs and peppers outside **your** kitchen for the freshest flavors possible.*

Ingredients:

2 large fresh eggs (lightly beaten) **or** 8 oz diced, firm-style Tofu
2 tablespoons low-fat milk (optional addition to eggs)
1 teaspoon olive oil
1/4 cup fresh grated sharp cheddar cheese
1 teaspoon chopped black olives
1 tablespoon fresh chopped cilantro
1/4 teaspoon fresh chopped oregano leaves (or 1/8 teaspoon dry)
Dash coriander (to taste)
1 fresh jalapeno or anaheim chile, chopped finely
3 mushrooms, cleaned and chopped
1 tablespoon *salsa* (of your choice)
1 small tomato, diced
1 tablespoon *light* sour cream
1 large vegetarian flour tortilla or 2 small corn tortillas

Heat the oil in a large skillet on medium-high heat until bubbling. Immediately turn heat down to medium and add eggs or tofu (or a combination of the two, if you choose). Stir with a fork until cooked to your taste. Add chiles, herbs, mushrooms, tomato, olives. Continue to stir constantly until mushrooms are slightly browned (just a minute or two). Lift this blend with a large spatula and slide tortilla under it. Place egg blend on top of tortilla and add the rest of the ingredients. If you are using corn tortillas, divide egg blend in half and place half on each tortilla. Fold corn or flour tortilla in half and cook about two minutes on each side, until cheese inside is melted. Serve immediately. Delicious!

Optional additions include cooked rice or refried beans, also good on the side.

Serves: 2

LEMON THYME TEA BREAD

Ingredients:

3/4 cup milk (whole or 2%)
1 heaping tablespoon fresh lemon thyme
   leaves (Finely chopped)
2 teaspoons lemon balm (finely chopped)
2 cups whole wheat flour
1 1/2 teaspoons baking powder
6 tablespoons butter
1 cup sugar
2 eggs
2 tablespoons lemon zest

Heat the milk with the herbs. Steep until cool. Mix flour with baking powder. In a separate bowl cream butter and sugar. Beat in eggs and lemon zest. Add flour mix and milk alternately until blended. Pour into a baking pan (bread pan or muffin pan can be used). Bake 50 minutes at 350 degrees.

Makes: 1 Small loaf or 12 small muffins.

BREAKFAST CHEESE SPREAD

If you love cream cheese on your bagels, toast or muffins in the morning, try this low-fat, delicious alternative!

Ingredients

2 heaping tablespoons low-fat ricotta cheese
2 teaspoons no-alcohol vanilla extract
1/2 teaspoon pumpkin pie spice or cinnamon

Mix all ingredients together until creamy. Also great on top of cinnamon-raisin toast. Spread on bread and put under the broiler until bubbly. (Be careful...it burns easily).

BREAKFAST SHORTCAKES

This recipe offers a very quick yet hearty and healthy way to start a busy day!

Ingredients

1 large muffin (try blueberry-bran, oat bran or any favorite muffin)
1 cup sliced fresh fruit (berries, melon, bananas, strawberries, etc.)
1/2 cup favortie flavor non-fat yogurt.

Slice muffin into 4 equal slices. Mix fruit and yogurt together. Layer muffin, fruit mix, repeat. Muffin slices can be toasted first if you like.

APRICOT BRAN MUFFINS

Ingredients

2 cups all bran
2 cups boiling water (mix with all bran & let soak while you work)
1 1/2 cups sugar
1 cup vegetable shortening
4 eggs
5 teaspoons baking soda
1 teaspoon salt (optional)
1 pint buttermilk
4 cups all bran
5 cups whole wheat pastry flour (substitute half white flour for lighter muffins)
3 cups dried apricot bits (substitute 1 cup mixed currents and chopped dates as a variation)

Combine all ingredients. Pour into lightly greased muffin pan and bake at 350 degrees for 25 minutes. Recipe will make 12 large or 24 small muffins.

BETTY'S GREAT GRANOLA

This recipe comes courtesy of my mother-in-law, Betty, who makes the most outrageous granola I have ever tasted. Not being much of a breakfast person, I am always searching for the ideal morning meal that will entice me to start the day in a healthy fashion. This is it!

Ingredients

5 cups old fashioned oats
1 cup sesame seeds
1 cup wheat germ
1 cup soy powder
1 cup shredded cocoanut
1 cup sunflower seeds
1 cup slivered almonds
1 cup chopped hazel nuts (this is the secret ingredient!)
1 cup honey
1 cup canola oil
1 cup mixed dried fruit of your choice
(raisins, dates, currents, apricots, etc)

Mix oil with honey. Combine all other ingredients in a large bowl and pour liquid over. Mix well. Pour mixture into a large baking pan and spread evenly. Bake in a 300 degree oven for 30 minutes, stirring every 5 minutes. Cool and add dried fruit. Serve with milk or as a trail mix. Recipe yields about 12 cups of cereal.

MAMA'S RICE AND POTATO CAKES

"Mama" was my grandmother and she had a fantastic way of turning left-overs into special treats. This recipe was one of her standards and remains one of my favorites to this day. These cakes can be prepared with rice, potatoes, bulgar wheat or couscous. They are a delightful way to turn left-overs into a hearty and delicious breakfast, or they can be the main course for lunch or dinner. No longer will you sigh at the thought of what to do with that half a pan of rice or potatoes after dinner!

Ingredients

2/3 cup cooked rice, mashed potatoes, bulgar wheat or couscous (or a combination of any) (Add slightly more or less grain depending on the desired consistency of the cakes)
1 egg
1 teaspoon olive oil
1/2 teaspoon Tobasco
1/2 teaspoon tamari
1/4 cup chopped green onions
Juice of 1/4 fresh lime
Optional: dash of dill, black pepper to taste, 1/8 teaspoon celery seeds, chopped roasted peppers (all according to your taste)

Garnish:
Salsa, dollop of sour cream, guacamole or sliced avocado, sliced olives-
OR- if you prefer sweet breakfast cakes, use honey, yogurt, applesauce or maple syrup (if you choose the sweet route, eliminate the onions and options above)

Heat oil in heavy skillet on medium-high. Mix all ingredients, including options, in a bowl until smooth using a wooden spoon or wire whisk. When oil sizzles, turn heat down to medium and pour grain and egg mix into skillet. Cook this fairly large pancake until browned and flip. Cook on the flip side until well done and nicely browned. Top with desired garnishes and serve piping hot.

Serves: One recipe makes one large pancake. Double, triple, etc. as desired.

TOFU PEPPER SCRAMBLE

This recipe is the great alternative to scrambled eggs, though hardly a sacrifice in any way. It provides protein and calcium without the fat and cholesterol of eggs and, best of all, tastes great and even looks pretty on the plate. I have often prepared this dish for food demonstrations since it is colorful and highlights my hot chile oil product . The variety of public responses has been incredibly entertaining. If people are told that the dish they're about to sample is "Tofu," many turn up their nose and won't even try it. So, I've made it a point not to tell what's in it before they taste. Reactions to the "mystery food" have been overwhelmingly positive. But, most people (those not familiar with tofu, that is) guess that it's some new kind of egg, chicken, turkey or cheese. One man, sporting a baseball cap that read "Eat Beef!" said "It tastes real good, darlin', but it's no wonder you're so darn skinny if this rabbit food is all you eat. Buy yourself a nice thick steak and you'll feel better!" He left with a bottle of the chile oil and a recipe card for the Tofu Scramble! The highest of praise!

Ingredients

1 pound firm style tofu, well drained
1 green bell pepper (cut in narrow, 1 inch strips)
1 yellow bell pepper (cut as above)
1 red bell pepper (cut as above)
1 small onion (chopped)
1 small clove garlic, minced
1 teaspoon herbed olive oil (herb blend to suite your taste)
1 teaspoon hot chile oil (more or less according to your affinity for heat)
2-4 individual red chiles from the bottle of oil
dash tamari to taste
dash dry white wine to taste

Heat the oil in a heavy skillet until sizzling (medium heat). Cut tofu into large chunks and, using your fingers, crumble the chunks into the skillet. Add onion, garlic, tamari and wine and cook (stirring occasionally) until the tofu gets slightly crisp around the edges. This takes about 7-8 minutes and the tofu will not crumble any further at this point. Add balance of ingredients and stir often for 3-4 minutes more. Do not overcook or peppers will lose their color and flavor. Remove and serve immediately with fresh fruit, toast, tortillas or bagels.

Serves: 2-3

TOFU AVOCADO CHILAQUILES

"Chilaquiles" (pronounced "Chee-la-`key-lace") is a traditional Mexican scrambled egg dish with many delightful variations. This recipe substitutes tofu for the eggs, but it is also delicious with a combination of eggs and tofu or just with eggs, for traditionalists! Serve these Chilaquiles with Mimosas, black beans and tortillas and garnish with lime wedges and you won't find better south of the border.

Ingredients

1 pound firm style tofu (well drained)
1-2 beaten eggs (optional)
1 large ripe avocado (cut into thin slices)
5 small, fresh corn tortillas
1/2 cup grated Oaxacan white cheese (if available; if not, substitute sharp cheddar)
1 small onion (chopped)
4-6 small Anaheim peppers (finely chopped)
1 teaspoon herbed olive oil
dash Tobasco to taste
1 teaspoon hot chile oil (optional for more heat)

Heat the oils in a heavy skillet (medium-high heat) until sizzling. Hand crumble the tofu into the skilled and stir. Reduce heat to medium. Add onion and saute until clear. Slice the fresh tortillas into triangular wedges and add to skillet, thoroughly yet gently mixing with the tofu and onions. Add peppers and mix. Stir and cook 2-3 more minutes. Add cheese and cook just until melted on top (do not stir any further). Remove from heat, garnish with sliced avocado and serve. Provide lime wedges and salsa on the side with additional corn tortillas, black beans and, the perfect accompaniment, Mimosas made with fresh ornage juice.

Serves: 2-3 (4 if eggs are added)

APPETIZERS

Many of these recipes make great side dishes and even main dishes when light fare is in order. Use your imagination and these appetizers will be much more than chips and dip!

MUSHROOM MOUSSE

My mother always serves a beautiful crab mousse for company. She makes a separate little mousse for me since I don't eat the crab, which is how this recipe came about. Guests always want to taste mine and inevitably like it better! The original recipe calls for unflavored gelatin for which we have substituted arrowroot. So, you will find this mousse not quite as "moussey" as if it had the gelatin. If you don't mind eating gelatin (most vegetarians do mind) you can add 1 packet of gelatin instead of the arrowroot. Either way, the result is so good that the temptation to spoil one's dinner is severe!

Ingredients

3 Tablespoons hot water
2 Tablespoons arrowroot
1 cup finely chopped celery
1/2 small onion, finely chopped
1 cup mayonaise (or Nasoya Nayonasie made
  from tofu.)
1 can mushroom soup
12 fresh button mushrooms (chopped into
tiny bits)
juice of 1/2 fresh lemon
6 oz softened cream cheese

Dissolve the arrowroot in the water. Heat mushroom soup until hot, **not** boiling. Add arrowroot . Remove from heat. Combine mayonaise cream cheese and lemon juice. Beat until very smooth. Add to cooled soup mixture. Add celery , onion and fresh mushrooms and mix. Pour into very lightly greased mold (grease with light oil then wipe with paper towel). Chill for 6 hours before serving. Garnish with fresh parsley. Serve with chips, crackers, sliced veggies and/or sliced sourdough baguette.

Serves: 6-8

CHIVE AND CHEESE WONTONS WITH HOT MUSTARD

These special wontons take more time than most other hors d' oeuvres in this chapter so plan to serve them when you have time to prepare them in advance (or on the rare day when you have plenty of time before a dinner party and want to play with the appetizers!). They can be prepared and refrigerated one day in advance and then heated before serving. They are scrumptious, beautiful and well worth the effort. Be sure to save a few for the cook!

Ingredients

1 package small (3-4 inch square) wonton
  skins (contains approximately 50 skins)
1 large stalk celery (finely chopped)
1 bunch onion chives (finely cut with scissors)
1/2 pound extra sharp cheddar cheese (grated)
small glass water for dipping fingers
skillet or wok filled with 2 inches canola oil
  for frying
roll paper towels
1 jar Chinese-style HOT mustard

Toss grated cheese with celery and chives, thoroughly mixing. Lay out wonton skins on a large bread board. Place a teaspoonful of cheese mix in the center of each wonton skin. Dip one finger in water and wet just the edge of a skin. Fold skin in half, sealing edges completely. (The edges will glue themselves together with pressure when wet). Repeat until all skins are filled and sealed. Prepare a large platter covered with paper towels near stove. Heat oil in skillet or wok on high until bubbling. Hold a slotted spoon in one hand and drop one skin at a time into the oil. As soon as the skin hits the hot oil it will puff up and begin to brown on the outside. Remove it immediately and drain as much oil through spoon as possible. Place skin on paper towel and repeat process until all skins are cooked. Serve immediately with hot mustard for dipping or refrigerate and re-heat in the oven (do not microwave) prior to serving. Do not keep for more than 24 hours (they get soggy in the refrigerator after this time).
Serves: 6 (approx. 5 wontons each)

OLIVE-HERB CAVIAR

Ingredients:

2 cans chopped black olives, drained
1 tsp. ground red chiles or prepared chile
  powder
2 small cloves garlic, minced
Juice of 1/2 lemon
1 tablespoon herbed olive oil (choose herbs
  according to taste)
1 tablespoon herbal vinegar (cilantro & garlic
  is ideal)
2 tablespoons fresh chopped cilantro
1 tablespoon fresh chopped onion chives
1 small can garbonzos

Garnish:
6-8 fresh lemons, thinly sliced
pickled ginger
pimentos
1 bunch green onions, finely chopped

For Dipping:
assorted chips, crackers, sliced sourdough
baguettes, veggies

In the blender place all ingredients. Blend until chunky-smoothe. Arrange blended mixture on platter and garnish according to taste.
Serve chilled.

Serves: 4 to 6.

HOT EGGPLANT, BASIL & GARLIC DIP

This is a new twist on an old Middle East favorite called "Baba Ganoush". It is delightfully quick and heavenly scented and flavored, so, be careful that your guests don't consume too much before the main course begins! It can be served with a green salad as a very light dinner on a hot summer night as it was the first time I tried it.

Ingredients:

1 medium size eggplant
1/4 cup packed fresh basil leaves
6-8 cloves garlic, minced (the dish is defi nitely for garlic lovers!)
1/2 cup herbed olive oil (basil flavored)
Juice of 1 lemon
1 package pita bread (6-8 pieces, cut in small triangles & lightly toasted for dipping)

Begin by washing eggplant and steaming or microwaving it (in a plastic bag with small air hole) until tender. Peel and cut into small chunks. Place in blender with basil, garlic, oil and lemon. Blend until smoothe. Lightly toast pita bread triangles to use for dipping. Serve piping hot.

Serves: 4-6.

SUN DRIED TOMATO AND HERB STUFFED MUSHROOMS

This is the appetizer that always disappears the fastest at any buffet table. If you are going to take it to a party, you may as well pre-print the recipe on 3x5 cards to hand out since everyone will ask you for it! The beauty of the recipe is that it can be varied in countless ways to accomodate personal taste and seasonal ingredients. Start with the cream cheese base and lovely, large, fresh mushrooms and you can't go wrong.

Ingredients:

20 large fresh Mushrooms
2 tablespoons fresh chopped Italian parsley
1/2 teaspoon fresh rosemary leaves (or 1/4 tsp. dry), crushed
1/2 teaspoon celery seed
1/2 teaspoon fresh lemon thyme leaves, crushed
1 tablespoon fresh onion chives, finely chopped
2 tablespoons minced sun dried tomatoes
16 oz. softened cream cheese
1 tablespoon mayonaise (or Nayonaise)
2 teaspoons olive oil (for sauteing mush rooms)
dash Tobasco (more to taste)
1/2 teaspoon curry powder (more to taste)
2 stalks celery, finely chopped
1 cup fresh grated parmesan (total for topping & filling)

Wash and dry mushrooms thoroughly. Place oil in large skillet on medium-high heat and saute mushrooms briefly (about 3-4 minutes, do not allow to soften).
Pat oil off mushrooms with a paper towel. Set aside to cool. Place cream cheese in a bowl and blend with mayonaise and 1/4 cup parmesan (set rest of parmesan aside for topping). Add all other ingredients and blend (ingredients should blend adequately with a wooden spoon). Using a small metal spoon, scoop filling into mushrooms, pack down, filling mushroom completely. Place mushrooms on a grilling pan that will fit under your broiler. Top each mushroom with a generous covering of parmesan. Just before serving, broil mushrooms until the parmesan begins to brown and bubble (about 10-15 minutes, depending on your broiler). Serve immediately. Tasty variations include adding finely chopped artichoke hearts, chopped seasoned olives, dash of lemon juice, pimentos...the list is as infinite as your imagination.
Serves: 7 combined with other hor d'oeuvres.

STUFFED MUSHROOMS VARIATION

Ingredients:

16 very large mushrooms (scrubbed,
de-stemmed & dried)
1-8 oz package cream cheese
1 teaspoon Tobasco (more or less to taste)
1/2 teaspoon curry powder
1 large stalk celery (chopped)
3-4 green onions (finely chopped greens only)
1 tablespoon mayonaise
1/2 cup freshly grated parmesan cheese
1 teaspoon olive oil (for saute)

Briefly sauté the mushrooms in very hot olive oil. Remove from saute and pat with paper towels. Set aside. Mix all ingredients, except the parmesan. Using a small spoon, fill the mushrooms with the cream cheese blend, packing them with the rounded back of the spoon. Lay the mushrooms on an ungreased baking sheet and sprinkle with the parmesan. Place under the broiler approximately 8-10 minutes prior to serving. Broil mushrooms until the tops are slightly browned and cheese is bubbly. Ideally these mushrooms should be served piping hot but they are so delicious that you won't have to worry about them sitting around getting cold!

Serves: 4 (depends on how many other appetizers are served)

GRILLED TEMPEH SKEWERS

A group of friends made these vegetarian shish kabobs for a Sunday picnic. The perfect finger food for appetizers they can also be removed from the skewers and served as a side dish for rice, lentils or noodles. The Hawaiian Papaya Salsa I suggest as the glaze is a new discovery I received as a gift from friends who recently moved to Kauai. It can be ordered directly from the small company which sells it. Contact: Papaya Mama— c/o Brie, P.O. Box 635, Kilauea, HI. 96754

Ingredients

2 16 oz. packages tempeh (a firm fermented
    style of tofu)
3 or 4 small zucchinis
12 large mushrooms
2 large red or brown onions
2 firm beefsteak tomatoes or four smaller
    ones
12 bamboo skewers

The Marinade/Glaze

Version #1
3/4 cup herbal vinegar—*dill preferred*
1 teaspoon mustard seed
1 teaspoon minced sun dried tomatoes

Cube tempeh and soak it overnight in a bowl with the above mix—if you are short on time a quick marinade of one hour will do. Save the vinegar mix for the glaze. Add 2 tablespoons margarine to the vinegar mix, heat in a small saucepan until margarine is melted and brush over skewers while cooking.

Version #2
Prepared Hawaiian Papaya Salsa serves as marinade and glaze (heat as above).

Cut all ingredients into bite-sized chunks (large enough to be skewered without falling apart.) Arrange them on the bamboo skewers in this order: tempeh, onion, zucchini, mushroom, tomato, tempeh, tomato, mushroom, zucchini, onion, tempeh. This process is a great group effort—be creative! The artists in the group will insist on restyling the skewers, that's ok! When complete, place skewers on the barbecue or on a cookie sheet for broiling in the oven. Brush each skewer with some glaze, cook until slightly browned, turn, glaze again and finish cooking.

Serves 6 (2 skewers each)

BLACK MUSTARD POTATOES

Ingredients:

10 small red potatoes (cleaned but not peeled)
1-8 oz jar German-syle black mustard
1 bunch onion chives (finely cut with
   scissors)
1-6 oz jar roasted bell peppers
1-8 oz jar stuffed green olives (stuffing of
   your choice)
1 box toothpicks (decorative if available)

Cover potatoes with water in a large pot. Cook until tender when tested with a fork. Drain and cool. When cool enough to handle, slice each potato in half. From the exact center of each half, carefully scoop out a hole using a small melon baller (available most grocery stores in utensil section). Sprinkle onion chives over potatoes, sparingly. Arrange potato halves on serving platter. Fill centers with black mustard (level, not heaping). Place one olive in the center of each. Place one small slice of roasted pepper on top of each olive and anchor with a toothpick. Be careful not to push mustard out of potato when putting the toothpick in. Toothpick can be used to pick up potatoes if pushed all the way into the potato. Chill thoroughly (at least one hour) prior to serving.

Serves: 5 (4 halves each)

EASY ARTICHOKES

These artichokes can be made in advance as they refrigerate well. They can be served as a hot or cold appetizer or as a main dish for a light supper.

Ingredients

2 large artichokes
1/2 cup mayonnaise (try new cholesterol-free varieties or Nayonaise
1/2 cup herbal or berry vinegar , seasoned according to taste.

Cook artichokes in boiling water (or steamer) until leaves pull off easily but are not mushy—*approx. 20 minutes*. When steaming hot, pour blended mayonnaise and vinegar over the top until the artichokes are completely soaked. Serve immediately or refrigerate for up to four days. (Try substituting yogurt or sour cream for the mayonaise as an alternative!)

Serves : 8 as an appetizer (1/4 artichoke each) or 2-4 as a side or main dish.

SALADS

These salads, like the appetizers, can easily substitute as a full meal. Feel free to play with them, adding seasonal favorites of your own and you will find that you can create a new salad for each day of the week... and never get tired of eating the healthiest of all foods!

AVOCADO-PAPAYA SALAD WITH PINE NUTS

A light, "almost fruity" salad, full of vitamins and minerals. The perfect complement to a rich or hearty main course,

The Salad

2 large ripe Haas avocados
2 medium size ripe papayas
1 bunch fresh spinach
1/2 cup pine nuts (unsalted)
1/4 cup pressed basil leaves *purple opal and or sweet basil*

The Dressing

1/4 cup herbal vinegar—*basil blend is good*
1/4 cup herbed olive oil—*basil, oregano, bay preferred*
Shake well.

or

Oriental Dressing

1/4 cup blueberry vinegar—*substitute raspberry or strawberry according to taste.*
1/4 cup sesame oil
1 tsp. grated fresh ginger
1 teaspoon. sesame seed—*dressing has a nutty, rich flavor*

Peel and cut the avocado and papaya into bite-size pieces. Wash and drain the basil and spinach leaves. Line a large salad bowl with the leaves—*about one inch thick.* Toss avocado, papaya and pinenuts together and pour into the center of the salad bowl lined with leaves. Salad portions should be dressed on the individual plates, not in the main bowl. This salad looks very beautiful at the table: especially colorful if you throw in a few purple opal basil leaves for contrast.

Serves 6

TICO'S FAVORITE PRIMATE SALAD

My friend Diana works as a volunteer at our local zoo. When I told her about a new salad recipe I had created she said, "That's Tico, the spider monkey's, favorite meal! That's the mix we feed the primates!" So we decided to give Tico credit for appreciating something humans don't often consider; the fact that fruits and greens can and should be mixed together. Hopefully, this recipe will give you a creative push—don't be afraid to experiment combining fruits and vegetables of all kinds.
Our relatives, the primates, know what's really good.

Ingredients

2 ripe bananas—*cut into bite sized pieces*
1 cup drained mandarin oranges
1/2 cup chopped walnuts
1 small bunch spinach—*cleaned and chopped*
1 small head red leaf lettuce—*cleaned and
    torn into bite-sized pieces.*
Unsweetened shredded coconut.

Toss all ingredients in a large salad bowl.
Add dressing, toss again and serve.

The Dressing

1 cup avocado or olive oil
1/2 cup raspberry or blueberry vinegar
2 tablespoons chopped scallions
1 teaspoon Dijon mustard
1/2 teaspoon whole mustard seed
1 teaspoon honey
Black pepper to taste

Mix all ingredients briefly on low in blender or stir well with wire whisk. This "Berry Vinaigrette" will keep for about two weeks in the refrigerator. Try it on all your favorite salads as well as on baked potatoes, french fries, steamed vegetables and artichokes.

Serves 4-6

NORTH AFRICAN CARROT SALAD

This ethnic version of the old standard "carrot salad" relies on the fresh, tangy flavors of a variety of herbs for its most unique character, taste and color.

Ingredients:

1 lb. fresh, tender carrots
2 cloves unpeeled garlic
2 tablespoons fresh lemon juice
3 tablespoons minced onion chives
2 tablespoons minced fresh dill
2 tablespoons minced fresh parsley
1 tablespoon olive oil
1/2 teaspoon cumin
1/4 teaspoon paprika
1/8 teaspoon ground cinnamon
Dash of cayenne pepper (to taste)

Bring 1 inch water to a boil in a saucepan. Put in the garlic and set steamer tray with carrots over water. Steam until tender-crisp. Put steamed carrots into a bowl and add chives, dill and parsley. Remove cloves of garlic from water. Peel and mash garlic and add it to lemon juice, oil and spices (blend or whisk). Stir into carrots and refrigerate until chilled.

Serves: 2 to 4.

ONION CHIVE TOFU SALAD with SEAWEED & WASABE

This light, richly flavored salad is perfect as a first course when served with Miso Soup and followed by any Asian main dish (see Lemon Thyme Tofu and Mixed Vegetable Chop Suey).

Ingredients:

1 lb. firm-style Tofu (Chinese Style)
1 bunch green onions (finely chopped)
1 bunch onion chives (finely chopped)
1 cucumber (peeled and sliced very thin)
1 package purple seaweed (*Porphyra sp.*) Can be found in Asian sections of most markets.
Wasabe powder (mix with water according to directions on package)
Tamari (soy sauce)
Herbal rice vinegar (choose a variety containing chives, garlic or parsley)
pickled ginger for garnish
toasted sesame seeds for garnish

Drain tofu and cube into bite-size pieces. Rinse the plastic tray that the tofu came in and cover the bottom with a thin layer of onion chives and green onions. Place tofu back into the plastic tray. Cover the tofu completely with the herbal vinegar. Cover and refrigerate over night. When ready to serve, remove tofu from tray and place in a large bowl. Pour about half the vinegar over the tofu, including the greens from the bottom of the tray. Float cucumber in the vinegar around the tofu. Add 2 tablespoons each of chives and onions, spreading it evenly over tofu. Crumble the seaweed (it will be dry and brittle in the package), or tear into small strips and sprinkle over tofu. This beautiful seaweed adds color and a slightly salty flavor to your salad. Use just enough to be visually pleasing, not the whole package. Sprinkle a light covering of sesame seeds and pickled ginger over tofu. Mix Wasabe and Tamari at a ratio that suits your taste. A 1:1 ratio will be very hot; add more tamari and less wasabe for milder flavor. This mix will be for dipping the tofu cubes just before eating. Tofu salad of this kind is easiest to eat with chop sticks. It is excellent when accompanied by hot Saké and/or and imported Asian beer.
Serves: 2

ORANGE SPINACH & BASIL SALAD
with Hot Garlic Dressing

The hot dressing for this salad is what gives it a lovely flavor and "wilted" quality. The dressing is a variation on the Herb Vinaigrette so prepare that recipe first.

Ingredients:

1 large bunch spinach (carefully cleaned)
1 bunch fresh basil (about 12 leaves)
1 small can Mandarin orange slices (no syrup)
1/4 cup slivered almonds
6 large sliced mushrooms
6 cloves garlic (minced) more or less to taste
soy bits for garnish
herbed croutons for garnish
1 recipe Herb Vinaigrette dressing (see pg.36)

Drain and dry spinach and basil and place in a large salad bowl. Add mushrooms, almonds, oranges and toss well. Add minced garlic to the Herb Vinaigrette dressing and heat over low heat until almost boiling, remove and stir thoroughly. Pour over salad just before serving, toss. Garnish with soy bits and croutons.* See recipe pg. 39.

Serves: 4

The best packaged croutons come from New York City! Contact:
Cousins Krutons, Inc.
163 Amsterdam Ave. Ste. 156
NYC, NY 10023

SALADE POMME DE TERRE

"Pomme de terre" literally translated means "apple of the ground" ....a strange thing to call a potato, perhaps, but a delicious staple that provides the base for this classic French salad and many other wonderful dishes. I discovered this salad while traveling in France on about a dollar a day. One of its many beauties is its low cost! Another is the fact that it makes a large quantity, delightful for picnics or sack lunches. It does not include mayonaise in the base and so does not have to be refrigerated nor does it have any cholesterol.

Ingredients

4 large red potatoes (about 2 1/2 lbs)
1 small red onion (chopped)
1/3 cup chopped fresh parsley
1 Tablespoon dijon mustard
1 teaspoon tamari
1/2 teaspoon black pepper
1 teaspoon tarragon leaves
1-2 cloves garlic (pressed)
1/2 cup herbal vinegar (lemon thyme if available. Otherwise choose a seasonal blend to ....suit your taste.)
2/3 cup herbed olive oil (parsley, chives and/or celery seed)
2 Tablespoons minced sun dried tomatoes packed in olive oil
1 heaping teaspoon capers

Place potatoes in 1 inch boiling water. Cover and cook until tender when pierced with a fork (about 30 minutes). You can also microwave the potatoes 10-14 min., depending on your oven. Drain, let stand for 10 minutes and dice into small cubes. Do not peel.

Place potatoes in a large salad bowl. Add parsley and onions. Blend together mustard and balance of ingredients. Pour over potato mixture and toss gently to coat. Cover and let stand at room temperature for a few hours before serving. You may chill if desired but the salad is really meant to be served at room temperature and the flavors emerge beautifully unchilled.

Serves: 8

SMORGASBORD OF HERBAL DRESSINGS

The dressings described here will be used with some of the salads to follow. Try serving a luncheon or light supper party with a buffet of all the salads and dressings and home baked breads (see recipe for Lemon Thyme Tea Bread & Herbed Yogurt Cheese). Dressings and salads can be mixed and mingled for fantastic new taste treats. Always include a basic mixed green salad in addition to the more unusual salads described here.

HERBED YOGURT DRESSING

1 cup plain yogurt
6 tablespoons fresh lemon juice
1 tablespoon canola oil
6 tablespoons chopped fresh herbs
(your choice of herbs, try: basil, oregano, bay; chives, celery seed, parsley; dill, parsley , thyme, chervil)
Combine in bowl, mix until creamy with a whisk or electric mixer.

LEMON-DILL MAYONAISE

This dressing contains one third the calories of regular mayonaise! It is also very adaptable to a variety of tastes. Try substituting other herbs and flavors of your own.

Ingredients:

1 egg
2 tablespoons fresh lemon juice
2 tablespoons fresh chopped dill (or 1 tablespoon dry dill weed)
2 tablespoons canola oil
1 teaspoon Dijon mustard
1 clove garlic, minced
1 cup part skim ricotta cheese
Blend on high until mixed. Refrigerate.

CREAMY TARRAGON DRESSING

1 teaspoon Dijon mustard
2 tablespoons Lemon-Dill Mayonaise
2 tablespoons Tarragon Herb Vinegar
2 tablespoons canola oil
2 tablespoons olive oil
1 tablespoon minced fresh tarragon
1 tablespoon minced fresh parsley

In a small bowl whisk together mayo and mustard. Add vinegar and whisk. Slowly whisk in oil. Stir in herbs until blended.

HERBAL VINAIGRETTE WITH SUN DRIED TOMATOES

2 tablespoons plain rice vinegar
2 teaspoons balsamic vinegar
2 tablespoons fresh lemon juice
1/3 cup canola oil
1/3 cup olive oil
1 teaspoon tamari
1 tablespoon dry dill weed
2 tablespoons fresh chopped cilantro
2 tablespoons minced sun dried tomatoes
1 teaspoon mustard seed
Dash cayenne pepper (to taste)

Whisk together until completely blended or use blender.

LIME VINAIGRETTE SALAD DRESSING

Ingredients:

3/4 cup herbed olive oil (dill & hot chile is
  best)
1/4 cup fresh lime juice
1/4 cup herbal vinegar (your choice of herbs)
1 clove crushed garlic
1 tablespoon capers
1 tablespoon chopped green onions
1 tablespoon fresh, finely chopped Italian
  parsley

Blend all ingredients in the blender or shake in a closed jar. Store under refrigeration. Dressing will keep a minimum of two weeks.

Recipe makes approximately 1 1/2 cup dressing.

ANGEL HAIR PASTA with FRESH TOMATOES & BASIL
Served with Creamy Tarragon Dressing

This delicately flavored salad is a great main course for lunch or a light dinner with garlic bread. It can be served hot or cold and its flavor improves with age, so, make the full recipe even if you only want one serving. Leftovers will be most welcome!

Ingredients:

1 lb. Angel Hair Pasta
6-8 large ripe Roma tomatoes (fresh)
8 oz. mozarella cheese
1/2 cup packed fresh basil leaves
12 leaves fresh rosemary (individual leaves, not stems)
1/4 cup fresh grated parmesan cheese for topping
1 tablespoon capers
1 recipe Creamy Tarragon Dressing (see pg.36)

Bring 4 quarts water to a rapid boil and add tomatoes. Cook them until the skin cracks (just a couple of minutes), immediately remove with a slotted spoon, cool slightly and peel. Add pasta to boiling water and cook "al dente". Chop tomatoes into chunks and mix in a large bowl with drained pasta. Chop basil leaves and add to pasta with rosemary leaves. Add capers and cubed mozzarella. Toss well. Add Creamy Tarragon Dressing (about 3/4 cup) and toss just to coat pasta. Serve at room temperature, topped with parmesan. If you wish to heat leftovers, do so in the microwave so that all flavor is retained.

Serves: 4 hungry people

GARLIC AND PESTO CROUTONS

These are quick and easy, inexpensive, fresh-tasting croutons you can make at home to give salads a very special gourmet quality. There are very few commercial croutons that will taste as good. One of the few is produced by a company called Cousins Krutons in New York City, difficult to find on the West Coast , so far. Their address is on pg. 33, but I much prefer to make my own.

Ingredients:

1 Loaf unsliced Sourdough bread (cut into 1 1/2 - 2 inch squares)
4 cloves minced garlic
1 stick butter or margarine

Prepared basil pesto (your own, or commercial quality pesto. Christopher Ranch makes a good one).

GARLIC VERSION:

Toast the bread squares in the oven until they are crunchy. Melt the butter and mix with the minced garlic. Place the toasted squares on a baking sheet and drizzle the garlic blend over them, covering but not soaking. Keep blending the garlic and butter so that the garlic is evenly distributed. Put the baking sheet under the broiler and cook the croutons until they are sizzling but not browned. Remove. It will be tempting to eat the croutons fresh from the oven but try to save some for the salad!

PESTO VERSION:

Follow the above directions for the toasted sourdough squares. Place squares on baking sheet and "paint" pesto (using a pastry brush) onto top and sides. Broil as above.

SOUPS

When it comes to soups, I must depart a bit from the "quick & easy" theme. These soups are easy but most of them have to cook for quite awhile. This is one meal category that is really worth the time. Fresh soups are so delicious, so healthful and so complete as a meal that the time spent letting them cook is an investment that really pays off.

The recipes in this chapter make large quantities that can be frozen to provide many quick hot lunches and easy suppers for the future. I usually make soups on a day when I have lots of chores to do at home anyway. I put the soup on to cook (or use a crock pot) and with just a few occasional checks and stirs, it cooks without much thought. The result is a wonderful hearty meal and lots of "fast food" for the busy weeks ahead.

Once you have sampled even one of these home made soups it will be very difficult to go the "canned" route again. Of course, with busy schedules as they are, everyone resorts to the can once in awhile! Every time I do, all I can think of is the heavenly scent and fresh taste of my own soups and canned will never be the same!

MISO SOUP

This soup is a very simple, healthful and quick addition to any Asian style meal. It can accompany any of the Szechuan recipes found in the "Main Dish" chapter. This soup is high in protein and calcium with virtually no calories....tasty too!

Ingredients

1/2 teaspoon miso (a powder or paste made from barley or soy. Available at Health Food stores.)

1 1/2 tablespoons tamari—*natural soy sauce*

1 cup water.

1/8 teaspoon minced ginger—*fresh if available.*

1 small clove garlic—*minced*

Pinch of cayenne

1 teaspoon dry kelp—*the purple seaweed,* Porphyra *can be found in sheets in small packets in the oriental food section of most markets.* Crumble kelp between fingers, then measure.

1/2 stalk celery—*cut into tiny pieces.*

4 oz. firm style tofu—*cut into tiny pieces.*

More or less tofu can be added according to individual tastes. 8 oz. equals about 1/4 a standard commercial package of tofu.

4 thinly sliced fresh mushrooms.

Add a few dried chiles for a spicy version.

Mix miso with a small amount of the water, then combine with balance of ingredients. Cook over medium heat until celery becomes slightly tender. Soup should be very thin, like broth. Add water if necessary. Serve piping hot.

The traditional Japanese way of serving Miso Soup is in small bowls—the soup is sipped like a drink. The small pieces of tofu and celery can be eaten with chop-sticks. The Asian dishes found in this book are primarily Chinese and miso is used in thicker form as a broth over vegetables. This is a very versatile soup/sauce open for experimentation.

Serves one.

MISO BROTH (AS A SAUCE)

Use the recipe for Miso Soup, omitting celery, tofu and mushrooms and adding 2 1/2 teaspoons arrowroot . Add the miso broth to vegetables when they are almost finished cooking and allow to thicken.

CUBAN BLACK BEAN SOUP

Ingredients

8 oz. dry black beans
1 small onion—*chopped*
1 carrot—*chopped*
1/2 cup red wine
1/8 teaspoon Tobasco
1 tablespoon hot chile oil
1 clove garlic
1 tablespoon tamari
1/8 teaspoon cumin
2 tablespoons fresh cilantro
4 tablespoons margarine
Juice of 1 lemon
3 quarts water

Garnish

Sour cream
Guacamole
Fresh cilantro
Sliced limes

Wash beans thoroughly. Rinse 3 times. Cover with water. Add balance of ingredients and cook over medium heat for 1 hour. Lower heat and cook for an additional two hours or until beans are completely tender. Add water according to desired consistency. Pour into bowls and garnish with a slice of fresh lime, a dollop of sour cream and a dollop of guacamole (see recipe pg.   ) Add a fresh cilantro leaf for color. Soup freezes well, microwaves easily to re-heat.

Serves 8 or more.

SHERRIED CARROT AND PARSLEY SOUP

Ingredients:

8 medium size, tender carrots
1 small onion
4 tablespoons butter
1 1/2 cups buttermilk
1 tablespoon fresh chopped Italian parsley
1/4 teaspoon dry dill weed
3 tablespoons flour
1/4 cup sherry
dash of salt (optional)
2 dashes Tobasco
1 fresh lemon
4-6 fresh sprigs of mint (garnish)

Peel and dice carrots. Place in a large saucepan with enough water to cover. Cook over medium heat until tender. While the carrots are cooking, melt butter in medium saucepan and add finely chopped onion. Simmer over very low heat until onion is clear and tender - do not allow to brown. Slowly sift in the flour, mixing thoroughly. Allow to cook slightly (30 seconds or so) over very low heat. Gradually add the buttermilk, stirring constantly with a whisk. Continue cooking until mixture is smooth. Place the cooked carrots in blender and puree until smooth. Save the water from the cooked carrots - set aside. In small amounts, add the sauce mixture to the carrots in the blender. Add wine and mix. If the mixture is thicker than you wish, add a portion of the water from carrots. Return the entire mix to the large saucepan, adding tobasco, dill and salt (optional). Simmer until served. Can be refrigerated and reheated.
Garnish with lemon and mint.

Serves: 4 to 6

AVOCADO SOUP with SAGE CILANTRO SAUCE

Ingredients:

3 large Haas avocados (ripe)
2 tablespoons fresh lemon juice
1/2 teaspoon coriander
2 fresh jalapeno peppers (seeded and chopped finely)
dash Tobasco (to taste)
dash salt (to taste, optional)
1 cup yogurt
1 tablespoon sour cream
3 cups water

Sauce Ingredients:

3 tablespoons fresh chopped cilantro
1 tablespoon fresh chopped sage
3 tablespoons pine nuts
1/2 cup yogurt
1 tablespoon heavy cream
1/2 cup chopped red bell pepper (Garnish)

Peel and pit the avocados and puree in the blender with the lemon juice. Add all ingredients except water and blend until smooth. With blender running, add water and blend on "whip" setting until thoroughly mixed. Cover and chill before serving (2-3 hours).

Place cilantro, sage and pine nuts in blender and puree until fairly smooth. Slowly add yogurt and heavy cream and blend well.

To serve pour soup into bowls, garnish with red peppers and drizzle with sauce.

Serves: 6

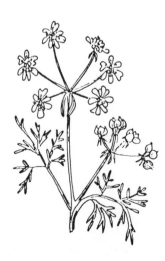

POTATO LEEK DILL SOUP

When I first grew leeks, I loved how fast they grew and how healthy they looked, but I hadn't really used them in cooking so my mother came up with this great soup that showcases them beautifully. Leeks have a mild, subtle flavor that is a welcome addition to all potato dishes.

Ingredients

4 medium size potatoes
1 fresh leek (bulb & greens)
  Clean & chop. Use tender part of
  greens and discard tips.
2 stalks celery (cut in 1" pieces)
1 small onion (chopped)
1 large carrot (chopped)
4 Tablespoons butter
2 "dashes" Tobasco
1/4 teaspoons dill
1/2 teaspoon dry basil or 2 tsp. fresh
3 tablespoons dry white wine
1 cup milk (low fat optional)

Peel and dice potatoes. Add celery, leeks, onions, carrots with potatoes to a large soup pot. Cover with 3 quarts water. Add balance of ingredients (except milk). Cook over medium heat until potatoes are completely tender (about 30 min.). Using a potato masher or pastry blender mash potatoes slightly. Continue cooking for another 15 minutes. Add milk in small amounts until a creamy texture is created (to suit your taste). Simmer until ready to serve. Garnish with fresh chopped Italian parsley.

Serves 8.

ICE BERG SOUP

Ice berg lettuce is not the first thing a gourmet produce shopper will think of reaching for! This recipe may change some minds! Here is a quick and easy soup that makes extraordinary use of this ordinary lettuce. It also provides some unique left-over possibilities.

Ingredients

1 head ice berg lettuce
1 package firm style tofu
1 brown onion
12 fresh mushrooms
tamari to taste
1 teaspoon dill
1/2 teaspoon celery seed
3 tablespoons olive oil (dill flavored if available)
1/4 cup dry white wine
1.9 oz. dry mushroom soup mix (1 package, all vegetable base)
1 Tablespoon cultured buttermilk powder
4-5 dry red Santaka chile pods (substitute any hot dry red chile if not available)
sour cream (garnish option)
fresh onion chives (garnish option)

Place olive oil in a large skillet on medium-high setting. When it begins to bubble, add chopped onion, sliced mushrooms and dried, sliced tofu. Stir and cook mixture until onions are clear. Dissolve mushroom soup , add to skillet and transfer blend to a large soup pan. Add 6 cups water and bring to a boil. Shred lettuce and add to boiling pot. Add balance of ingredients and reduce heat to medium. Cook until lettuce is very tender and soup has thickened slightly (to desired consistency). About 30-45 minutes, stirring occasionally. Soup can be garnished with dollop of sour cream and chopped onion chives.

Serves: 8

ICE BERG LEFT-OVERS

CURRIED SOUP SANDWICH

Ingredients

Left-over soup (cooked down or with liquid
    drained off)
1 tablespoon mayonaise (or Nayonaise)
1/4 teaspoon curry powder
1/2 cup peanuts
1/4 cup shredded cocoanut

Place all ingredients in blender and blend until
chunky-smooth. Use as you would egg salad
for sandwiches.

ICE BERG TOMATO SALAD

Core and hollow large, beefsteak tomatoes and
fill with Curried Soup Sandwich mix.Top with
a squirt of fresh lemon juice.

ICE BERG DIP

Heat Curried Soup Sandwich mix in small
sauce pan or microwave and serve with
vegetable sticks or chips. Be ready to give
out the recipe if you take it to a party!

SOUP OF GREENS

This is the quickest, freshest soup imaginable. If you plan to have a summer garden, plant accordingly. It is an especially nice way to use those prolific zucchini plants!

Ingredients:

1 pound green beans
4 stalks celery
6 sliced zucchini
1/2 cup packed fresh Italian parsley
1/2 cup packed fresh basil
1 green bell pepper
1 vegetable boullion cube
1/4 cup dry white wine
Juice of 1/2 fresh lime
1/2 teaspoon Tobasco
tamari to taste
lemon pepper to taste

Put 1 1/2 quart water into large soup pot, add boullion cube and bring to a boil. Add beans, celery and bell pepper and boil for 3 minutes. Reduce heat and add balance of ingredients. Cook for 5 more minutes. Remove from heat and pour into blender, blending to desired consistency. Return to heat if necessary before serving.

Serves: 4 -6

MAIN DISHES

In this chapter you will find pastas and sauces, luncheon foods, casseroles and simple dinners of all kinds. As always, the emphasis is on flexibility and creativity. These recipes can be combined with all the soups, salads and appetizers and finished off with a great dessert for a delightful smorgasbord of beauty and taste. Or, they can be served very simply and easily all by themselves.

MELINDA'S CLASSIC VEGGIE BURGERS

My friend, Melinda, is a wizard of a cook and a walking herb encyclopedia! This is my favorite of all the delightful recipes she contributed to this book. This burger mix is also great in tacos and in pita bread instead of felafel.

Ingredients:

1 cup chopped walnuts
1 pound grated sharp cheddar cheese
1 onion, minced
2 cups cooked brown rice (or a combination
   of cooked wild rice, wheat berries and
   brown rice)
1 cup grated carrots
4 eggs (beaten)
1 Tablespoon tamari
1 Tablespoon minced garlic

Seasoning Options (choose one): 1 teaspoon each cumin and chile powder (more or less to taste)

or

1 Tablespoon herb blend (finely minced & mixed: rosemary, thyme, marjoram, sage, onion chives)

Mix all ingredients (including seasoning choice) in a large bowl. Form into patties and fry in a little oil in a non-stick pan; or, bake in an oiled loaf pan for 45 minutes in a 350 degree oven. Serve with your favorite "burger" condiments.

Serves: 4-8 depending on pattie size

ORANGE CREAM PASTA WITH SPRING FLOWERS

This is a delightfully rich, subtly flavored pasta and makes a wonderful main dish for dinner, but can also be served for brunch. The secret to the delicate herb flavors is to carefully mince the lavender and chive flowers so that no large pieces remain. Garnish creatively with any other edible flowers you have — nasturtium, thyme, mint, lemon balm, etc.

The Sauce

1 cup chopped walnuts

7 oz. olive oil

1 1/2 cup half and half

1/4 cup cream

1 cup *fresh* orange juice

Zest of one orange (finely grated rind, only the orange part, not the white)

2 cans (11 oz.) Mandarin Oranges (completely drained)

8 fresh onions chive flowers (substitute dried chives 2 Tablespoons and 1 teaspoon crushed red pepper if fresh flowers not available)

6 *dried* lavender flowers (fresh flowers taste bitter)

1/4 cup dry white wine

1/4 cup brandy or Gran Marnie

The Pasta

Cooked *al dente* (firm to the bite, 5-6 minutes)

18 oz. fresh linguine

The Garnish

Grated fresh Parmesan

Chopped walnuts

Fresh Bergamot leaves (orange mint)

Directions next page

Orange Cream Pasta continued:

In a mixer, place the walnuts and oil. Blend on "chop" until thoroughly mixed. Pour into a large skillet (preferably cast iron) and place on medium heat. Add half and half, cream, orange juice, zest...stirring continuously with a wire whisk. Continue stirring and add the wine and brandy. Heat until sauce begins to bubble. Turn heat down to medium-low. Chop the mandarin oranges into small segments and add to sauce. Stir to blend. Sauce will tend to separate when not being stirred.* Turn heat down to low and continue to cook while pasta is prepared. Cook pasta *al dente.* Drain pasta and add finely minced chives and lavender to sauce. Toss sauce with pasta in large bowl. Dress with freshly grated Parmesan, chopped walnuts and fresh Bergamot. All to taste.

This recipe is a fairly thin sauce, but will thicken as it cooks. Heat longer for thicker sauce, stirring often. If you have your own lavender plants (easy to grow) just pinch off a handful of flowers and dry them in a clean warm spot for about a week before using. If you don't have freshly dried lavender, it is not essential. The recipe is great without it!

Excellent served with Avocado and Papaya Salad or with Oriental Orange Spinach Salad. See recipes, pg.
Serves 6. Small portions recommended

SPEEDY-SPICY-SPINACH CASSEROLE

This recipe makes a large hearty casserole. It can be taken to work and eaten as a cold rice salad or mixed with greens—salad dressing adds a nice touch to this lunch leftover. It tastes even better the second night if re-heated for dinner.

Ingredients

1 package frozen spinach

1 box brown and wild rice mix—*instant*
   (Read label to avoid preservatives & animal fat.)

1 package firm style tofu (about 16 oz.)

1 cup chopped fresh mushrooms

4 cloves fresh garlic

3 tablespoons herbed olive oil—*basil, oregano, and bay are good*

4 tablespoons minced sun-dried tomato (packed in olive oil)

1 teaspoon hot chile oil

1 small onion, chopped

1/2 cup grated fresh Parmesan cheese

Prepare the rice first as it can cook while you work on the rest of the casserole. In a large, heavy skillet, place the oils, garlic, onion and sun-dried tomatoes. *Saute* until the onions are clear, making sure not to burn the tomatoes. Add extra olive oil if necessary to prevent drying of mixture. Add mushrooms and tofu (cut into bite size chunks) and continue to *saute* until tofu is coated with the color of the oil mix. Stir occasionally. Frozen spinach can be defrosted quickly in the microwave or in advance if you have time. Drain it completely and mix with the *saute* blend in a large casserole dish. Add Parmesan and rice and mix again. Bake in a 350 degree oven for 30 minutes in a covered casserole

Serves 6 hungry people.

LINGUINI with CREAMY FRESH HERB MEDLEY SAUCE

Ingredients:

12 oz. fresh linguini (cooked, al dente, and
   drained)
4 tablespoons fresh chopped basil
2 tablespoons fresh chopped oregano leaves
2 tablespoons fresh chopped Italian or curly
   leaf parsley
2 teaspoons fresh chopped dill
1 teaspoon fresh chopped mint leaves
2 tablespoons olive oil
8 cloves garlic (finely chopped)
1 cup cream
black pepper to taste
freshly grated parmesan for garnish

Saute garlic in oil until browned. Mix herbs briefly with oil and garlic. Toss cooked pasta with herb mix in skillet. Over low heat, slowly add cream while stirring pasta. When sauce has reached desired consistency (add more or less cream as needed), add pepper to taste, remove from heat, garnish with parmesan and serve.

Serves: 4

CHINESE HERB PASTA

Hot and spicy, this pasta makes a great main dish or a unique side dish to accompany any oriental main dish. Vary ginger and hot chiles according to your taste for the flame!

Ingredients:

1 tablespoon fresh chopped cilantro
1 tablespoon fresh chopped basil
1 tablespoon fresh chopped parsley
1 tablespoon fresh grated ginger
2 tablespoon tamari (soy sauce)
5 cloves minced garlic
2 tablespoon hot chile oil (Santaka preferable)
2-3 hot dried chiles (from oil)
1 tablespoon dark sesame oil (oriental)
1 tablespoon plain or herbal rice vinegar
1 bunch green onions (garnish)
1 tablespoon sesame seeds (garnish)
1 small onion (chopped)
1/2 cup sliced mushrooms
1/2 cup chopped broccoli
1 cup snow peas
1/2 cup water chestnuts
12-16 oz. wide egg noodles (dried)

Saute onion and garlic in oils, slowly adding vinegar, tamari, ginger, herbs then vegetables. Cook pasta al dente while veggies are tenderizing. Continue to cook saute blend until vegetables are tender-crisp (about 10 min. over medium heat). Drain pasta and toss with vegetable-herb saute. Garnish with sesame seeds and chopped green onions.

SPICY TOFU with HOT PEANUT CILANTRO SAUCE

This unusual treatment of tofu gets its spice from hot chiles and its Indonesian peanut-herb sauce. It makes a great side dish served with plain steamed broccoli, green beans or green squash or serve it as a main course over brown rice or pasta. Vary the heat according to your taste (adding more or less hot chile oil and crused chiles). The dish should ideally be cooked in a wok, but, if you don't have one a large cast iron skillet will do.

Ingredients:

1 lb. firm style tofu
3 tablespoons sesame oil
1 teaspoon hot chile oil
1 heaping tablespoon peanut butter
1/2 teaspoon crushed red chiles
1 teaspoon tamari (more to taste)
1 tablespoon fresh cilantro (finely chopped)
2 teaspoons fresh chopped onion chives
sesame seeds (for garnish)

In the wok place the oils over medium-high heat. When bubbly, add peanut butter and crushed chiles and stir until smooth. Lower heat to medium. Add tamari, chives and cilantro, stir well. Add tofu and toss. Continue to cook until tofu has absorbed plenty of sauce (it will have an even brown coating). Serve over brown rice or noodles or as a side dish to vegetables. Garnish with a sprinkle of sesame seeds.

Serves: 4-6

FLOWERING CHIVE STUFFED PEPPERS

Onion chives are really fun to grow and their pink flowers are as decorative as they are tasty. Try planting some chive plants along the edges of a walkway or in pots by the kitchen door. They are very hearty and require little care. They reseed freely so you can count on a bigger crop each year without replanting. When your chives begin to flower, try this great stuffed pepper recipe to experience the spicy, peppery seasoning provided by the prettiest part of your plants.

Ingredients:

4 very large bell peppers (yellow, red or green—try all 3!)
1-15 oz can of spicy, vegetarian chile (available health food stores)
1 cup freshly cooked brown rice
1/2 cup crumbled feta cheese
1/2 cup cubed firm-style tofu
1/4 cup fresh cut onion chives (cut into small pieces with scissors)
1/4 cup fresh onion chive flowers (separated into tiny bits)
1 cup fresh onion chive flowers (left whole)

Preheat oven to 375 degrees. Cut off tops of peppers and cut out stems and seeds. Put peppers into a large pot of boiling water for exactly 5 minutes. Remove and drain. Put peppers into a glass baking dish. In a large bowl combine rest of ingredients, setting aside the whole chive flowers. Spoon mixture into peppers until filled. Bake for 15-20 minutes, until cheese is completely melted. Top each cooked pepper with a few of the whole chive flowers for decoration. These peppers are a hearty meal so serve with a large green salad for a full dinner.

Serves: 4 (double all ingredients for 8)

TWICE BAKED DILL POTATOES

It's not just the dill that gives these potatoes such a distinct flavor. The dill is dominant, but the other herbs combine to provide a complex secondary flavor that is so delightful you may decide to serve this otherwise ordinary dish as a featured entre at your next party. Serve with simple steamed vegetables and salad or with the whole Salad Buffet as a complete banquet.

Ingredients:

3 large brown potatoes (thoroughly baked)
1 tablespoon fresh chopped dill leaves
1 teaspoon fresh chopped parsley
1/2 teaspoon fresh crushed rosemary leaves
1 teaspoon fresh chopped onion chives
1 small onion (minced)
4 tablespoons butter
1/2 cup sour cream or plain yogurt
1/4 cup grated sharp cheddar cheese

Thoroughly bake potatoes, remove from oven and leave it on at 350 degrees. Slice baked potatoes in half , scoop out insides (leaving skin in good condition!), and mash. Saute the onion in the butter until clear. Add chopped herbs (all stems removed) and stir briefly. Pour onion-herb blend into mashed potatoes. Mix in the sour cream or yogurt and the cheese. Refill the potato skins and bake 20-30 minutes.

Serves: 6 as a side dish or 3 as entre.

MUSHROOM HERB LOAF
(The "I'm-afraid-to-call-it-lentil-loaf-or-no-one-will-try-it" Loaf)

What's the first thing a non-vegetarian thinks of when having a vegetarian to dinner? "Lentil Loaf!" The result is that the poor vegetarian is usually subjected to a ten pound lump of tasteless "spam-like substance". Well, no longer! This is a delicious rendition of the traditional "Loaf" that can be served hot or cold. It even makes great sandwiches!

Ingredients

1/2 cup whole wheat bread crumbs
1/2 tablespoon soy mineral bouillon (Dr. Bronner's works)
1/4 cup soy granules
1/4 teaspoon salt
1/8 cup milk
1 large onion, chopped
1 large stalk celery, chopped
1 egg (beaten)
1/3 cup tomato juice
1 pound fresh mushrooms (sliced)
2 cloves garlic (minced)
2 tablespoons olive oil
1 teaspoon dried basil
1/2 teaspoon cayenne pepper
1 small red onion, chopped
1/4 cup dry white wine

In a large saucepan, cook soy granules in 1/2 cup water with salt until nearly dry. Add balance of first nine ingredients and mix well. Lightly oil a loaf pan and bake 1 hour at 325 degrees. While the loaf is baking, saute the sliced mushrooms in a skillet with the garlic, olive oil, basil, cayenne, onion and wine. When the loaf comes out of the oven, let it cool slightly, slice and top with the mushroom saute.

Serves: 4; thickness of slices will vary according to taste.

PURPLE QUESADILLAS

The "purple" in these quesadillas comes from purple cabbage which gives them a refreshing twist. Shred the cabbage as you would for cole slaw before beginning.

Ingredients:

4 fresh corn tortillas (for 2quesadillas)
1/4 small purple cabbage head
1/2 cup shredded cheese or soy cheese
1 tablespoon diced jalapeno peppers
1/4 cup diced green onions
1 fresh tomato, diced (or substitute fresh
   tomato salsa)
fresh tomato salsa for topping
sour cream (optional) for topping
guacamole (optional) for topping

In a no-stick pan on medium-high heat, place one tortilla covered with one layer each of : cheese, cabbage, tomatoes or salsa, onions, jalapenos. Cover with another tortilla. Reduce heat to medium and cook until cheese begins to melt. Using a spatula, flip the tortilla sandwich over and cook on the other side just until cheese has completely melted.

Remove from heat. Keep warm in oven while next quesadilla is prepared. If you are lucky enough to have a grill, you can cook both at once. Top with salsa, guacamole and/or sour cream. Slice quesadilla into halves or quarters so that it's easy to pick up and so that the lovely purple color shows.

Serves: 2 (double recipe as desired)

GINGER ASPARAGUS STIR-FRY WITH COUSCOUS

Although designed to go with couscous, this recipe is also wonderful with pasta, rice or bulgar wheat. Use your imagination (try potatoes as well!) and save yourself a trip to the store by using what you have on hand. Don't forget to save left-over grains for breakfast cakes!

Ingredients

1 box couscous (cook according to instruc tions. Near East brand is good)
24 young, tender spears of asparagus (about 1 "bunch" in the market)
1/4 cup chopped green onions
2 heaping tablespoons pickled ginger (finely chopped)
1/2 cup roasted unsalted peanuts
3 large cloves garlic (minced)
half of 1 large fresh lime
2 tablespoons olive oil (use herbed oil if available)
2 tablespoons sesame seeds
2 tablespoons chopped fresh cilantrodash tamari (to taste)
1/2 teaspoon Tobasco (more or less to taste)
dash dry white wine (to taste)

Optional additions:
3/4 cup sliced purple cabbage
1/2 pound diced firm style tofu
1 cup fresh chopped spinach
1/2 cup fresh grated parmesan cheese

Heat oil in heavy skillet or wok on medium-high heat until sizzling. Add garlic, sesame seeds and optional tofu and saute until slightly browned, stirring constantly. Add balance of ingredients and cook until asparagus is just tender (do not overcook). Add spinach and purple cabbage last if you are using it. Total cooking time will be approximately ten minutes. Skillet or wok can be covered to steam the asparagus and optional spinach for just a minute or so. When ready, serve piping hot with couscous. Top with optional grated parmesan if desired. Pasta, rice or bulgar wheat can be substituted for the couscous if you wish.

Serves: 2-4 (depending on options added)

PAN PICANTE

This Mexican style "spoon" corn bread is very filling. It makes the perfect accompaniment to any of our soups, salads or light dishes; especially the Cuban Black Bean Soup.

Ingredients:

1 package cornbread mix (*Marie Callendar* makes a high quality commercial mix or find a good one at the health food store)

2 1/4 cup non-fat milk

1/2 cup Hot Chile & Dill herbed olive oil

1-12 oz can creamed corn

1 1/2 cups grated sharp cheddar cheese

1 large grated onion

1 large can diced green chiles

3/4 cup hot salsa

1/2 teaspoon cumin

1/2 cup packed, chopped fresh cilantro

1/2 cup chopped green onion

3 beaten eggs (add last)

Preheat oven to 450 degrees. Mix all ingredients together in a large bowl, adding eggs last. Lightly grease a 9x12 inch baking dish and pour in bread batter. Bake for 35-45 minutes, according to oven. Top will be very browned. Bread will have a very creamy texture, but will cut into squares with a very cold knife.

Serves: 8

CURRIED CARROTS

One year we had a particularly large crop of sweet little carrots in the garden and, searching for new ways to use them, discovered this very quick recipe for a colorful and delicious side dish. For a light supper, try these carrots as a main dish served with green salad and toasted sour dough bread.

Ingredients

12 very fresh, tender carrots
1 teaspoon butter or margarine
1/2 teaspoon dill
1/2 teaspoon curry powder
1/4 cup sour cream (vary quantity for desired
    consistency of puree)
Fresh parsley for garnish

Steam carrots just until tender (do not overcook), 3-5 minutes. Place in blender with balance of ingredients and blend until smooth. Garnish with fresh parsley sprigs and serve immediately.

PRONTO CHILE MOLE

This recipe for quick, homemade, Mexican-style chile is medium spicy as written. You can accomodate your taste for the flame by varying these ingredients: chile powder, dried hot chiles (Santakas) and/or hot chile oil.

The word "mole" (pronounced `mow-lay), refers to the traditional use of chocolate in sauces. Mole sauce is more popular in some regions of Mexico than the typical red or green sauces we find in the US. The mole sauces of Mexico vary in sweetness, thickness and heat but are all rich in flavor. If you like the hint of chocolate in this chile, experiment the next time you make enchiladas or any Mexican dish with a sauce. You can often find canned mole sauce in Mexican food sections in grocery stores, but of course it will not be as good as your own!

Ingredients:

4 large red onions
1 large green bell pepper
1 tablespoon hot chile oil
1 tablespoon cocoa powder (semi sweet)
1 tablespoon chile powder
1 Tablespoon brown mustard
1 teaspoon cumin seeds
1/4 teaspoon ground cinnamon
1 large (16 oz) can chopped tomatoes
24 oz. cooked kidney beans, undrained (38 oz
   cans or measure fresh cooked)
1 cup water
1 6 oz can tomato paste
4-6 dry Santaka chiles (optional) use any dry,
   hot, red chile if Santaka aren't available
Toppings: (optional)
low-fat, plain yogurt
sour cream
grated cheddar cheese

In a large kettle or dutch oven, cook onions and green pepper in oil over medium-high heat, stirring occasionally until onions are golden and pepper is soft. Add mustard, chile powder, cumin, cocoa, cinnamon, tomatoes (with liquid), beans(with liquid) and tomato paste. Add additional hot dried chiles if desired. Reduce heat and simmer uncovered for about 40 minutes until most of the liquid has cooked away and chile is thick. Stir frequently to prevent burning. Top each serving with a dollop of plain, low-fat yogurt or sour cream and grated cheddar (optional). Serve with a green salad and warm tortillas or Pan Picante (see recipe, Pg.65).

Serves: 6 (probably with left-overs)

EASY CHEEZY TACOS with FRESH TOMATO SALSA

Ingredients:

12 corn tortillas
2 cups grated sharp cheddar and/or Oaxacan
   cheese(loosely packed)
1 small can chopped black olives
1 cup chopped green onions
1/2 cup sliced jalapeno peppers
1 large fresh tomato (chopped)
1/2 cup sour cream
1 container alfalfa or mixed sprouts
2 cups (approx.) shredded lettuce
Salsa (pg. 69)
sliced avacado

Quantities of ingredients are approximate because you will fill these tacos as you go and you can make big, fat ones, or little, thin ones. Using a non-stick pan, heat one tortilla until it is soft and pliable. Sprinkle with a thin layer of cheese followed by a sprinkling (about 1 teaspoonful) of olives, onions, peppers and tomatoes. Fold tortilla in half and cook, on both sides, until shell is crispy (or softer, according to preference). Repeat until all tacos are made. Keep tacos warm in oven while you work. Fill tacos with lettuce and sprouts and top with sour cream, fresh tomato salsa and sliced avacado. *Maravillosos!*

Serves: 4 (3 tacos each)

FRESH TOMATO SALSA

Ingredients

5 cups fresh tomatoes (chopped)

2 cups fresh peppers (chopped, mix hot &
   mild according to taste)

1 cup chopped onion

4 cloves pressed garlic

2 tablespoons fresh lime juice

dash herbal vinegar (any blend)

2 tablespoons fresh chopped cilantro

1 tablespoon fresh chopped Italian parsley

1/2 teaspoon oregano (optional)

1/2 teaspoon cumin (optional)

Place all ingredients in a saucepan and bring to a boil over medium high heat. Remove from heat and let stand until cool or serve warm. Refrigerates for about one week.

CHILE RELLENO CASSEROLE with GUACAMOLE

Ingredients:

8-10 roasted pasilla chiles (fresh roasted or 2
   cans of preroasted)
1 tablespoon flour
3 eggs
1 cup Oaxacan white cheese (Jack will work
   as a substitute)
1 cup sharpcheddar cheese
3 tablespoons milk

The Topping:

1 large (very ripe) avocado
3 green onions (finely diced)
juice of 1/2 fresh lemon
3 dashes Tobasco
1 large tomato

Preheat oven to 375 degrees. Lightly grease a large baking dish. Split chiles, rinse and remove center strips and seeds. Mix 2 types grated cheeses together, setting 1/2 cup aside for later. Fill chiles with cheese, using toothpicks to secure if necessary. Place in baking dish. Separate eggs. Beat whites until very stiff. Beat yellows separately adding the milk. Gently fold into the egg whites. Spoon mixture over the chiles. Top with balance of the grated cheese. Bake in preheated oven for 45 minutes (should be puffy and slightly brown). While the casserole is baking, peel the avocado and mash with a fork. Add the lemon juice and Tobasco. Peel the tomato, remove seeds and dice into small pieces. Add the tomato and the onion to the guacamole. When casserole is done, remove toothpicks and serve topped with guacamole. Dish should be served piping hot. Green salad, brown rice, tortillas, refried beans and lime wedges make great accompaniments.

Serves: 4-5 (2 rellenos each)

CHINESE FOOD

The recipes for the Chinese foods which follow come, with my greatest thanks, from the best Chinese-style cook I know, Janet Storey. Though she is now an architect in Montana and her name as a chef may not be well known, anyone who has ever eaten in the Almond Cookie Cafe in Santa Cruz, California, will know what I'm talking about. Janet was the first vegetarian in our group of friends, over twenty years ago. She has always introduced me to cutting- edge trends in cooking. She opened the Almond Cookie Cafe in 1978 in response to fans of her Szechuan and Cantonese stylings. Though the cafe closed when Janet decided to become an architect (she could always do anything she set her mind to!) her recipes have lived on in my kitchen all these years and I am thrilled to be able to include them in this book.

Janet had her own form of oriental wisdom which she developed along with her recipes. It had to do with the mystery of stocking the oriental kitchen. Chinatown in San Francisco (especially Stockton St.) remains our favorite place to shop for ingredients and cookware, however, in most cities where "Chinatowns" exist you will be able to find specialized foods. As today's grocery stores expand their ethnic food sections, oriental specialty foods are becoming more common as well. When shopping in any of these markets, keep your eyes open for deals on authentic chopsticks, woks, tea sets, dishes, black mushrooms, fresh snow peas, fresh ginger, green teas, imported beers and fresh water chestnuts. One of Janet's favorite cooking "pearls" was, "Be brave! Experiment!" So, try something new each time you shop...and have a great time with these Chinese recipes.

CHINESE FOOD BASICS

THE RICE...Traditional white rice can be used with the following recipes, but the much preferred choice for a healthier, happier result is the brown rice recipe below.

THE MISO... see page 43 (SOUPS) for Recipe.

Ingredients

1 cup short grain brown rice (uncooked)
1 1/2 cup water
1 tablespoon plus 1 teaspoon tamari

Place all ingredients in a large sauce pan and bring to a boil. Turn heat down to simmer for 35-40 minutes, until water is absorbed and rice is tender (stir occasionally). If the rice should burn and stick to the pan, never fear! According to *Zen Macrobiotic Cooking* by George Osawa, the blackened rice is supposed to be particularly good for you! Ideally, however, burned rice is not as tasty and can be avoided by an occasional stir. Be sure to add water as the rice cooks if it begins to stick to the pan.

SERVES: 4 (1/2 cup servings)

VEGETABLE CHOP SUEY

Ingredients

1 serving miso broth (see pg. 43)

2 tablespoons peanut or safflower oil

1/4 cup chopped onions

1 cup chopped celery

1/2 cup sliced mushrooms

1 cup diagonally cut bok choy or chopped
swiss chard

1 cup chopped cabbage (green or purple)

3/4 lb. bean sprouts (Mung sprouts are
available in most markets)

Sesame seeds to taste

Heat oil in wok*. Saute onions for one minute then add the rest of the vegetables. Stir fry for 4-5 minutes or until sprouts are tender. Add miso broth and allow to thicken. Sprinkle with sesame seeds and serve with brown rice (or the traditional Chinese white rice).

*About woks: A 12" steel wok is ideal for stir-frying. It will require very little oil because of its sloped sides and cooks food very quickly. After using the wok, be sure to scrub it or wipe clean with a paper towel. Re-oil the wok if necessary so that it won't rust. If you don't have a wok, a skillet will do (use slightly more oil and cook a little longer). Ideally a heavy, cast iron skillet should be used.

Serves: 2

SNOW PEA CHOP SUEY

A SIDE OF TOFU

Follow the Vegetable Chop Suey recipe—
sauté with the onions— add 1/4 pound fresh
snow peas...

Continue as directed.

TOFU CHOP SUEY

Follow the Vegetable Chop Suey recipe,
adding:

...1/2 lb. cubed firm style tofu (at the same
time you add vegetables)

Complete recipe as directed.

Ingredients

1 tablespoon sesame oil
1/4 cup fresh chopped green onions
1/2 pound firm style tofu
1/2 recipe Miso Broth

Sauté onions in oil for 1 minute. Add tofu and
broth. Thicken and serve. May also be served
as a cold salad. Garnish with fresh or pickled
ginger.

TOFU & MIXED VEGETABLE CHOP SUEY

Ingredients

2 tablespoons peanut or safflower oil
1/4 cup chopped onions
1/2 cup chopped celery
1/2 cup sliced mushrooms
1/2 cup diagonally cut bok choy or chopped
  Swiss chard
1/2 cup chopped caggage
1/2 lb. bean sprouts
1 cup chopped broccoli
1/4 lb. snow peas
1/2 cup any combination of the following:
  -finely sliced carrots
  -squash (zucchini or summer)
  -waterchestnuts
  -bamboo shoots
  -cucumber
  -peanuts, almonds, cashews or walnuts
  (chopped)
1/2 lb. firm style tofu

Start with the basic chop suey recipe. With the onions, saute the broccoli, snowpeas and the combination ingredients. Add the tofu and the greens at the same time. Complete with miso broth, let thicken and garnish with sesame seeds. Serve with rice.

Serves: 2-4, increase by adding greater volume of vegetables to suit your taste

ALMOND DICED VEGETABLES

CASHEW TOFU

Use the vegetable chop suey recipe. Omit the sprouts, double the green vegetables and add:

...2 cups diced broccoli
...1/2 cup diced almonds

Complete the recipe and top with chopped almonds to serve.

Use the vegetable chop suey recipe. Omit the sprouts, double the green vegetables and add:

...2 cups diced broccoli
...1/2 cup cashews
...1/2 lb. cubed tofu

Complete recipe, top with cashews and serve.

HONEY SWEET AND SOUR SAUCE

Ingredients

1/2 cup fresh orange juice

3 tablespoons lemon juice

3 tablespoons lemongrass herbal vinegar
  substitute plain rice vinegar in a pinch

1/4 cup honey

1/4 lb. tomatoes, sliced in eighths

2 tablespoons water

1 tablespoon arrowroot

1 clove garlic, minced

pinch each of cayenne, chili powder & kelp

Mix arrowroot and water; add the rest of ingredients and bring to a boil while stirring. Simmer until sauce thickens. Pour over vegetables, tofu, etc., sprinkle with sesame seeds and serve.

Serves: 2. Double or triple as desired.

SWEET AND SOUR VEGETABLES

SWEET AND SOUR TOFU

Ingredients

2 tablespoons oil (1/2 sesame, 1/2 peanut)
1 cup red cabbage (chopped)
1 cup pineapple (cubed)
1 cup thinly sliced carrots
1 cup sliced green peppers
1/2 cup diagonally cut celery
1/4 cup thinly sliced onion

Heat oil in wok (or skillet). Stir fry veggies until carrots are tender. Pour sweet & sour sauce over veggies, sprinkle with sesame seeds and serve.

Serves: 2 . Double or triple as desired.

Use recipe for Sweet and Sour Vegetables and add:

...1/2 lb. firm style tofu.

Tofu makes an easy and delightful variation on the vegetable recipe.

TAHINI SAUCE

Ingredients

1 tablespoon tahini (sesame butter)
1 1/2 tablespoon tamari
1 tablespoon fresh lemon juice
1 Tablespoon plus 1 teaspoon arrowroot
1 1/2 cup water
1 clove garlic (minced)

Mix arrowroot with a small amount of the water. Add the rest of the ingredients, mixing well. Use this sauce with tofu and vegetable recipes in this chapter. Garnish with sesame seeds, almonds or cashews.

Serves: 2

CAULIFLOWER, BROCCOLI AND MUSHROOMS WITH TAHINI SAUCE

Ingredients

1/4 cup onions (chopped)
2 tablespoons peanut oil
1 1/2 cup broccoli (chopped)
1 1/2 cup cauliflower (chopped)
1 1/2 cup mushrooms, sliced
Sesame seeds to taste

Stir fry for 5 minutes or until broccoli is tender. Add tahini sauce, allow to thicken, add sesame seeds and serve.

SERVES: 2.

BROCCOLI, MUSHROOMS AND CABBAGE WITH TAHINI SAUCE

Ingredients

2 tablespoons peanut oil
1/4 cup onions
1 1/2 cups sliced broccoli
1 1/2 cups sliced mushrooms
2 cups chopped cabbage (purple or green)
sesame seeds to taste

Sauté onions, add the rest of the veggies. Cook for 5 minutes or until broccoli is tender. Add tahini sauce, allow to thicken, garnish and serve.

SERVES: 2.

SUMMER VEGETABLES WITH TAHINI SAUCE

Follow the Broccoli, Mushroom and Cabbage recipe and add:

...1/2 cup crookneck squash
...1/2 cup zucchini squash

Complete recipe as directed.

THREE CHOP SUEY FAVORITES

Fresh Water Chestnuts

Start with the vegetable chop suey recipe and add:

...1/4 lb. thinly sliced fresh water chestnuts. Use them skin and all. They're tasty and sweet.

Cook according to recipe.

Black Mushrooms

Start with the vegetable chop suey recipe and add:

...1 oz. dried black mushrooms (soaked in 1/2 cup hot water for 10 minutes). Slice them, discarding stems and add them to vegetable mix.
...Mix 1 teaspoon arrowroot with the soaking water and add to miso broth.

Complete cooking according to recipe.

Summer Squashes

Start with vegetable chop suey recipe and add:

...1/2 cup zucchini, quartered and thinly sliced
...1/2 cup crookneck squash, sliced

Cook per recipe.

KUNG PAO MIXED VEGETABLES

Ingredients

1/4 cup peanut oil
4*whole dried red chiles (Santaka or
    Chile de Arbol)
1 1/2 cup carrots (thinly sliced, 2-3" lengths)
1 1/2 cup thinly sliced broccoli
1/2 cup peanuts
1/2 cup sliced bamboo shoots
2*large cloves garlic (minced)
1*teaspoon fresh ginger (minced)
Large*pinch Szechwan peppercorns
1/4 cup green onions, chopped
1 cup sliced bell peppers
1 cup "matchstick" sliced cucumbers (like the
    carrots)
1 tablespoon lemon juice
1 tablespoon tamari

*Heat is controlled by the quantity of these items. This is a hot dish, so you may want to make it milder or hotter by varying quantities of these spices.

Cook peppers in oil until brown. Add: carrots, broccoli, peanuts, bamboo shoots. Cook for 3-4 minutes while adding garlic, ginger & peppercorns. Then add balance of ingredients. Cook for 3-4 minutes more or until carrots are tender. Add 1 serving of miso broth and allow to thicken. Top with peanuts and serve with brown rice.

Serves: 4

SPECIAL ITALIAN FOODS

The Italian foods that follow come from the classic traditions of the classic Italians I grew up with. Some of these dishes have been modernized (and vegetarianized) as they passed through several generations, but their true essence remains.

I have never had more fun eating as I had in my years at the "bouna tavola" (good table) of the Harrold and Cox family. Though I was not related, I felt truly Italian. As a result, there is a lot of sentiment and personality in these Italian recipes. There is no better way to learn about the joys of the kitchen (cuccina!) than to live and cook with Italians! I hope that this joy is contagious as you prepare the foods from this chapter! Mange con amore!

TOMATO BASIL SAUCE

These fast and fresh sauces are great low-calorie toppers for your favorite pastas!

Ingredients

1 tablespoon Italian herbed olive oil
1/4 cup chopped shallots
1 clove crushed garlic
3 cups fresh plum tomatoes (diced) **OR**
3 cups canned plum tomatoes (drain and dice)
1/4 cup chopped fresh basil
3 tablespoons chopped fresh Italian parsley
Fresh Parmesan or Romano cheese
—1 tablespoon per serving, grated

Heat 1/2 tablespoon oil in a large skillet. Add shallots and basil. Saute until translucent. Add tomatoes, basil, parsley and balance of oil. Cook 5-8 minutes. Add cooked pasta of your choice (good selections are tortellini, linguini or fettuccini) and toss with 1 tablespoon fresh grated cheese.

Serves: 4 (1/2 cup servings of sauce)

RICOTTA MUSHROOM SAUCE

Ingredients:

1 cup lowfat Ricotta cheese
1/4 cup grated Parmesan cheese
4 additional tablespoons parmesan
1/4 cup chopped fresh basil
3 Tablespoons fresh Italian parsley
1/2 pound thinly sliced mushrooms
black pepper (to taste)
nutmeg (to taste)
4 baby zucchinis

In a large skillet, mix Ricotta and 1/4 cup Parmesan cheeses, herbs and mushrooms and cook for five minutes. Season with pepper and nutmeg to your taste. Mix with cooked pasta of your choice (this sauce is a delightful substitute for traditional spaghetti sauce). Toss with additional Parmesan. Grate one fresh baby zucchini over each of four servings.

Serves: 4 (1/2 cup servings of sauce)

LASAGNA ROLL-UPS

Lasagna never looked so unique and was never so easy to make as in this version created by my friend, Lindee. Of course, growing up in an Italian household, it's difficult not to inherit some wonderfully creative ways of cooking! Lindee did just that and I was lucky enough to be along for the ride as I spent as much time with her family as I did with my own.

Ingredients

One package of lasagna noodles (at least 20 individual noodles)
16 oz. lowfat Ricotta cheese
1 package frozen chopped spinach (defrosted and well drained)
 -be sure to press out extra water
1/2 cup fresh grated Parmesan cheese
1/2 teaspoon grated nutmeg
1 egg (well beaten)

Cook lasagna noodles (al dente) according to package instructions. Combine balance of ingredients in a large bowl. Spread cooked noodles flat on a cookie sheet. Spread 1/3 cup filling mix evenly onto individual noodle and roll up. Place rolled noodles into a lightly oiled baking dish, curly side up. Cover with La Famiglia Marinara Sauce (recipe Pg. 87) and bake at 350 degrees for 45 minutes.

Serves: 5 (4 rolls/hungry person)

LA FAMIGLIA MARINARA

This recipe is dedicated to my great friend, Aida Harrold, Lindee's wonderfully Italian auntie. Aida loved Italy and all things Italian, especially the food. We shared some great times and some great ideas about food and life. Aida always told me "Lisa, whatever you do, you do well!" I know that she was at least right about my cooking and I wish she could see the results in this book, but, she died suddenly while I was writing. I know her spirit is out there somewhere, smelling this sauce and saying, "Que bella la marinara!".

Ingredients

1 tablespoon Italian herbed olive oil
3 cloves garlic (thinly sliced)
1 large can tomato paste
1 large can tomato puree (from Roma or Plum tomatoes)
1 teaspoon dry basil leaves (plus 6 large fresh leaves)
1 teaspoon oregano
1 cup water
1/2 pound fresh sliced mushrooms (optional)

Heat (medium high setting) oil in a large sauce pan. Add garlic and saute until golden. Remove garlic and discard. Reduce heat to medium. Add paste and puree, then basil and oregano, stirring until well blended. Add water. Add mushrooms now (optional). Stir and turn heat down to lowest setting. Cover with lid slightly ajar. Stir frequently to prevent sticking. Cook 1 1/2 hours.

This sauce gets better with age. It can be made in advance and refrigerated up to one week or it can be frozen and defrosted as desired.

Serves: 8 (served over 8 plates of spaghetti or pasta of your choice.) The recipe makes enough for a complete casserole of Lasagna Roll-ups or Stuffed Basil Shells. Always be sure not to drown pasta in sauce, flavors of both are important.

STUFFED BASIL SHELLS

Ingredients

1 large package jumbo pasta shells (at least 30 shells)
1 recipe La Famiglia Marinara Sauce
1 recipe Ricotta filling from Lasagna Roll-ups
1 cup firmly packed fresh basil leaves
1-2 tablespoons Italian herbed olive oil

Cook jumbo shells (al dente) according to package instructions. Drain well. Prepare the Ricotta filling. Place the fresh basil and 1 Tablespoon oil in blender. Blend until a paste is formed (add additional oil if paste is too thick). Mix paste (pesto) with Ricotta filling. Fill each shell with approximately 2 Tablespoons filling and place in a large, lightly oiled baking dish. When all shells are completed, cover (about 3/4 depth of shells) with marinara sauce and bake at 350 degrees for 45 minutes.

Serves: 6-8 (5 shells each for very hungry people)

SPINACH BASIL TOFU LASAGNA

This recipe is one of my mother's favorite ways of using the freshest of the summer garden harvest...tomatoes, basil, oregano and spinach are taken from garden to plate in a beautiful as well as mouth-watering and healthy presentation...easy, too! Delicious served with Rosemary Focaccia (see recipe, pg. 90) and a green salad.

Ingredients:

8 fresh Roma tomatoes
1 small onion (chopped)
1 cup plain tomato sauce
1/4 teaspoon salt (optional)
2 cloves garlic (minced)
2 cups firmly packed fresh spinach leaves
1 cup packed basil leaves
2 bay leaves (fresh or dry)
2 tablespoons fresh chopped oregano
1 lb. firm style tofu
2 tablespoons Italian herbed olive oil
1/4 cup red wine
1 package lasagne noodles (about 12 strips)
1/2 cup fresh grated parmesan cheese

Preheat oven to 400 degrees.

Bring one quart water to a rapid boil. Place fresh tomatoes in the boiling water just until skin breaks. Remove with slotted spoon, peel and chop. Save water. Pour olive oil into large skillet, add chopped onion and cook over medium-high heat until clear. Add chopped tomatoes, tomato sauce, garlic, herbs, salt (optional). Cook on medium-low heat, stirring often, for about 45 minutes. Lightly steam spinach leaves and set aside. Place tofu and red wine in the blender and mix until very smooth. Add three quarts water to water from tomatoes and bring to a rapid boil. Cook lasagne noodles al dente and drain. Do not allow to cool completely before layering. Lightly grease a casserole dish and place one layer of pasta in bottom. Top with one layer of spinach leaves, half the tomato sauce & half the tofu blend. Lightly sprinkle with parmesan and repeat layering process with balance of ingredients. Top final layer with sprinkling of parmesan. Insert knife on all sides of baking dish to evenly distribute sauce. Bake for 35-40 minutes (until bubbly and slightly browned).
Serves: 4-6

ROSEMARY FOCCACIA TORTAS

"Tortas" are little Italian sandwiches . This hearty herbed bread can be eaten by itself or used for sandwiches. For a unique and filling dinner, try it with pesto, sliced tomatoes and mozarella slices (heat until cheese begins to melt). Try grilling your sandwiches for extra flavor.

Ingredients:

2 tablespoons fresh, individual rosemary leaves
1/2 teaspoon dried basil
1/2 teaspoon dried oregano
2 packages active dry yeast
1 teaspoon sugar
1 3/4 cup lukewarm water
1/3 cup olive oil with extra for "drizzle"
1 1/2 teaspoon salt (optional)
5 cups unbleached flour
Sliced tomatoes, onions, olives (optional
   toppings)

Dissolve yeast and sugar in 1 cup water, let sit until foamy. In another bowl add remaining 3/4 cup water, olive oil and salt. Pour in yeast mixture. Blend in flour, 1 cup at a time, until dough comes together. Knead on a floured board 10 minutes, adding flour until dough is smooth and elastic. Put in an oiled bowl, turn to coat well, cover with towel. Let rise 1 hour, until doubled. Punch down dough, knead 5 minutes. Roll out to fit a pan (15 1/2 x 10 1/2). Let rise 15 minutes covered. Oil fingers and make impressions in dough, 1" apart. Let rise 1 hour. Preheat oven to 400 degrees. Drizzle dough with olive oil, sprinkle with herbs and optional veggies. Bake 15-20 minutes, until golden brown. Cut into squares and serve warm.

Makes: 8-10 individual pieces or 4 sandwiches, depending on size of cuts

PEPPER HERB POLENTA

This baked polenta casserole is excellent served hot or cold. The spicy red sauce also makes an excellent salsa for topping other dishes. This dish combines the best of Mexican and Italian flavors. Try grilling the Polenta and dipping in the sauce as a variation.

Ingredients:

For the Polenta:
6 cups water
2 cups corn meal
1/2 teaspoon salt (optional)
2 tablespoons olive oil
5 tablespoons unsalted butter(cut into chunks)
1/2 cup chopped fresh onion chives
1/2 cup chopped fresh cilantro
1/4 cup chopped fresh basil
1/2 cup chopped green onions
2 tablespoons diced jalapeno peppers
1/4 teaspoon cayenne pepper (more to taste)
1 cup grated sharp cheddar cheese

For the sauce:
4 tablespoons Italian herbed olive oil
1 tablespoon hot chile oil
2 16 oz. cans stewed tomatoe,s
1 medium onion (chopped)
2 tablespoons diced jalapenos
1/2 cup fresh chopped cilantro
1 teaspoon ground cumin
2 medium size zucchini squash (thinly sliced)
6-8 large mushrooms (thinly sliced)
1 cup sharp grated cheddar cheese (for topping)
Additional fresh chopped cilantro (for topping)
Sour cream, sliced black olives,additional jalapenos, hot sauce (for garnish)

over for directions...

92

Polenta continued:

Oil 2 shallow baking dishes. Boil water for
polenta, adding 1 tablespoon oil and salt to
water. Slowly add corn meal, stirring continually with a whisk to avoid lumps. Turn heat
down to medium-low and continue stirring
until corn meal is very thick . Turn heat off
and add cheese and balance of ingredients,
mixing thoroughly. Pour polenta mix into
baking dishes and let sit at room temperature
until it sets up (about 3 hours). Setting can be
accelerated by refrigeration.

While polenta is setting heat olive oil for
sauce in a large cast iron skillet. Add onion
and cook over medium-high heat until clear.
Add tomatoes and turn heat down to medium.
Add zucchini, mushrooms, cumin, cilantro and
jalapenos and continue to cook until zucchini
is tender. Cover skillet and cook an additional
15 minutes, stirring occasionally. Turn heat
off and let sauce sit covered while you prepare
the polenta for layering.

Slice firm polenta into squares or triangles.
Lightly oil a deep casserole dish. Place one
layer of the polenta pieces in bottom of dish.
Spoon one layer of sauce on top and cover
with thin layer of cheddar cheese. Repeat
layering with balance of ingredients. Cover
final layer with cheese, sprinkle a few diced
jalapenos and some sliced black olives (optional). Bake casserole for 30 minutes at 350
degrees (until bubbling hot). Remove from
oven and let sit for 5 minutes before cutting
into deep sections and serving. Have additional hot sauce and sour cream on hand for
garnishing as well as extra fresh cilantro.
Dish can be reheated nicely or served cold.
Serves: 6

PASTA VERANO

This is my verano (summer) version of pasta primavera (spring), since on the central coast of California we have very foggy summers and need colorful dishes like this one to brighten our days. Serve this pasta hot or cold and use your own imagination when adding fresh vegetables and seasonings. Take advantage of any fresh vegetables you happen to have in your own garden.

Ingredients:

1 pound corkscrew pasta
2 pounds Roma or plum tomatoes
1 large head of broccoli, broken into small
    flowerettes
1 pound fresh mushrooms
1 cup fresh green peas
1 red onion, chopped
1- 8 oz can sliced olives
1 cup fresh corn (sliced off the cob)
1 large red pepper, seeded and sliced
1 cup packed fresh torn basil leaves
1/4 cup Italian blend herbed olive oil
    (extra oil to coat cooked pasta)
1/2 cup Italian herbal vinegar
1 cup grated parmesan cheese

In a large soup pot bring 1 gallon water to a rapid boil. Drop tomatoes in for a few minutes until skin cracks. Remove immediately with a slotted spoon, leaving water boiling. In same water, cook pasta al dente. Drain pasta, pour into **large** pasta bowl. Coat with very thin layer of herbed olive oil and toss. Peel tomatoes, chop and add to pasta, toss. Steam all vegetables until slightly tender, about 5 minutes. Transfer vegetables to pasta bowl and toss. Add torn basil leaves and toss. Mix together remaining olive oil and herbal vinegar and pour over pasta. Toss again before serving. Top with parmesan. Serve with sourdough toast. with herbed oil for dipping.

Serves: 20 (approximately 1 cup serving size)

BROCCOLI RISSOTO

This recipe was developed to use some left over Famiglia Marinara sauce and became so popular that we now make the sauce just to accompany the Rissoto! "Rissoto" (pronounced ree-`so-toe) means rice in Italian and forms the base of the dish. It's a nice change-up from pasta. It makes a great light dinner served with garlic bread and salad.

Ingredients:

1 recipe La Famiglia Marinara sauce (if left over, heat to piping hot)
1 cup uncooked brown rice
2 cups water
1 clove minced garlic
2 cups fresh broccoli (chopped into small pieces)
1 cup grated fresh parmesan cheese

Bring the rice and water and garlic slowly to a boil. Reduce heat and cook approximately 30 minutes, until rice is almost finished cooking. Beat the rice mix with a whisk until it is creamy in texture. Add broccoli to pan and stir. Cook another 5 minutes, or until broccoli is tender. Add the marinara sauce and parmesan and stir. Serve immediately.

Serves: 2

DESSERTS

To some people, desserts are an automatic end to a meal. Far too often empty calories are consumed on top of a meal when people don't even care that much about what they are eating. In contrast, the desserts in this chapter are designed as a real splurge. They are perhaps a bit healthier than some; a concerted effort has been made to eliminate excessive use of sugar, cream, eggs, etc., but, not so completely that we spoil the "indulgence" of the great treat.

Dessert is part of the real fun of cooking and eating so try not to spoil it with guilt about calories. You will find the recipes in this chapter very unique. Enjoy them!

KIWI-PEAR PIE

This dessert is light and delicious and takes advantage of whatever seasonal fresh fruits are available. Just about any fruits can be substituted for those listed below but the ones chosen make a beautiful pie with delightfully well-rounded flavors.

Ingredients

Filling
1 6 oz. package instant vanilla pudding
1 3/4 cup milk
3 oz. whipped cream cheese
1 tablespoon brandy or rum.

Crust
3/4 box vanilla wafers—*finely crushed*
Make sure the wafers you buy don't contain animal shortening
3/4 cube melted margarine

Topping
2 fresh Anjou pears
2 kiwis
1 banana
2 apricots
1/2 cup drained mandarin oranges
1 cup sweet muscat wine
1/4 cup fresh grapes
Fresh whipped cream—*as desired*

Prepare the pie crust first.

Mix the vanilla wafers thoroughly with the melted margarine. Press firmly into a standard pie pan or quiche dish. Cook in a pre-heated oven (350 degrees) for about five minutes or until lightly browned.

Combine pudding and milk. Beat with electric mixer two minutes on medium speed. Add softened cream cheese, beat one minute. Add brandy or rum, mix briefly. Pour into cooled crust. Core and halve pears, and cook in a sauce pan with muscat wine until completely tender. You may choose to cook any dried fruit in this wine as well. Drain fruit and completely dry using paper towels. It is important to make sure as much moisture as possible is removed from the fruit or it will make the pie soggy. Slice the pears and other fruit and arrange on top of the pie using a pattern of concentric circles. Completely cover exposed custard with fruit. Garnish with whipped cream. Accompany with dry Alsatian-style Gewurztraminer or Muscat Canelli dessert wine.

Serves 6-8

MAYME B's RED CAKE WITH FROSTED MINT LEAVES

My mother remembers going to her best friend's house during the holidays hoping to get a taste of her mother Mayme's, special "red cake." To this day my mother says it is the best cake she has ever had. For years she searched for a similar recipe but could never find one. This year Mayme's grandson was going through some of her old file boxes and found a 3x5 card with a recipe hand written in fading pencil for Red Cake. Thank you, Mark! The cake is very simple and really pretty. Children love it because of its great color and wonderful taste, of course! The perfect party cake.

Be sure to make the mint leaves first.

Ingredients (Cake)

1 cup butter or margarine
1 1/2 cup sugar
2 eggs
1 oz. red food color
1 teaspoon salt
1 cup buttermilk
2 1/2 cups cake flour
1 teaspoon soda
1 tablespoon cocoa
1 teaspoon vinegar (apple cider)
1 teaspoon vanilla

Mix vinegar and soda. Let stand. Cream butter and sugar, add eggs. Make as paste of cocoa and a little of the food color. Add to the mixture, then add the rest of the food color. Add buttermilk, salt and flour. Mix. Stir soda and vinegar into mix; add vanilla and mix well. Pour into 2 pans (2x8). Bake at 350 degrees for 30 minutes. Cool then split layers.

Frosting

1 pint whipping cream
1 teaspoon vanilla
1 teaspoon sugar (more to taste)
1 teaspoon cinnamon

Whip cream, adding rest of ingredients, until if forms stiff peaks. Ice cake between layers, on sides and top.

Garnish (prepare first. Leaves will be ready to use by the time cake is frosted.)
24 favorite mint leaves (orange mint works well)
1 egg white
1/8 cup water
1/4 cup sugar (white, granulated)

Rinse and dry mint leaves (pat dry with paper towel.) Mix egg white and water in bowl. Dip mint leaves first in egg mix then in sugar, lightly coating both sides. Place them on a piece of wax paper to dry. When dry, mint leaves will be stiff. Arrange them on top of cake in a wreath pattern (or design of your choice.)

ROSEHIPS RICE PUDDING

Rosehips (red capsules that are the fruit of the rose bush) are naturally sweet, citrus flavored and high in vitamin C. They provide a unique flavor twist to this lovely pudding. Rosehips can be purchased whole or ground in many health food stores.

Ingredients:

3 1/2 cups milk (low fat is fine)

2 tablespoons butter or margarine

1/4 cup sugar

1/2 cup short grain brown rice (cooked)

1 vanilla bean (1/2" in length)

1 egg yolk

1 cinnamon stick

2 tablespoons purified water

3/4 cup raisins (try substituting or mixing
   dried cranberries as a variation)

1/2 cup (chopped or ground) rosehips

In a gallon sauce pan, place margarine, milk, sugar, rice, vanilla and cinnamon. Bring to a boil, reduce heat and simmer 8 minutes. Stir every couple of minutes. Combine egg yolk and water, then stir into saucepan. Simmer 10 minutes longer and remove from heat. Transfer to a separate bowl and chill. While in the refrigerator, stir occasionally to prevent rice from sticking to the bottom of the pan. Simmer raisins 3 minutes in water deep enough to cover them. Let them cool before mixing into pudding. Refrigerate 2-3 hours to cool, or serve warm. Top with ground cinnamon and a layer of rosehips.

Serves: 6 (1/4 cup servings)

BRANDIED CAROB-MINT BANANAS
with HONEYSUCKLE VANILLA ICE CREAM

Ingredients:

2 bananas (peeled and sliced down the middle in half)

2 teaspoons butter or margarine

2 teaspoons carob powder

1/8 teaspoon mint extract

12 small fresh mint leaves (preferably orange-mint)

2 tablespoons brandy (may also use Kahlua or Grand Marnier according to taste)

2 scoops vanilla ice cream

12 fresh honeysuckle flowers

Melt butter in large skillet over medium-high heat.

Turn heat down to medium and add bananas, flat side down. Sprinkle 1 teaspoon carob powder over tops of bananas. Cook until flat side is slightly browned. Turn bananas with spatula. Sprinkle flat side of bananas with remaining carob powder. When rounded side of bananas is slightly browned, add brandy and mint extract to skillet. Holding skillet by the handle, swizzle bananas around in the liquid. Add mint leaves to skillet, cook about 30 seconds longer and remove. Place 2 bananas on one plate and top with scoop of ice cream. Snip off tips of honeysuckle flowers so that "honey" will run out. Stick open tips of flowers into ice cream (6 per scoop). Honeysuckly liquid will flavor ice cream which will melt slightly over hot bananas. Outrageously decadent dessert!

Serves: 2 (one banana per person).

RICOTTA CHEESECAKE WITH MELBA SAUCE

Although cheesecake can never really be considered "low-fat", this one is low sugar and low-fat compared to most. None of the flavor or sinfulness of this wonderfully rich and creamy dessert is lost when you follow this recipe. The melba sauce is an optional topping but try it at least once—it is delightful ! If it is winter and fresh fruit is not available it can be prepared with frozen (check to see that no sugar has been added). Try the melba sauce as a topping on vanilla yogurt or ice cream as well.

Ingredients:

3 eggs
1/2 cup grated lemon rind
2 Tablespoons Amaretto liqueur
2 Tablespoons brown sugar
1 pound lowfat ricotta cheese
Melba sauce (optional)

Preheat oven to 350 degrees. Lightly butter and flour a 6 cup springform pan. Beat eggs with lemon rind in a large bowl. In a small saucepan, heat Amaretto and sugar for about 3 minutes. Blend into egg mix. Add ricotta and continue to beat. Transfer batter to pan and bake for 30 minutes. Remove from oven, let cool and run a knife around the edge to loosen. Remove the pan rim and slide cake onto a serving platter. Garnish with melba (Optional).

MELBA SAUCE

Use all raspberries to turn this sauce into a classic raspberry coulis. Use fresh fruit when seasonally available, frozen otherwise. This sauce is wonderful over any cake or pudding, ice cream, yogurt... you name it.

Ingredients:

1 1/4 cup peaches
1/2 cup apricots
1 1/4 cup raspberries
1 tablespoon corn starch
1 tablespoon water
2 tablespoons kirsch or chambord liqueur

Place all fruit in blender or food processor with steel blade. Blend well (chunky or smooth according to taste). Transfer to saucepan and heat on medium setting until it boils. Mix together the cornstarch and water and add to the fruit, stirring, cooking for 1 minute more until it thickens and looks clear. Remove from heat and strain (to remove raspberry seeds) the mix into a bowl. Stir in the liqueur and refrigerate for one hour before serving. Recipe makes about one cup of sauce.

FRESH BERRY TRIFLE

Ingredients:

1 loaf pound cake
1 basket fresh raspberries, blueberries or
    strawberries (or a combination)
4 oz fresh whipping cream (whipped)
1- 8 oz package vanilla pudding, prepared (or
    use Rosehips Rice Pudding pg. 99)
1/2 cup brandy
1/4 cup dark rum
1/8 cup Gran Marnier

Start with six parfait glasses or any tall, cylindrical glasses available. Using a stainless teaspoon, scoop spoonfuls of pound cake into the bottoms of the glasses, forming a layer about 1 inch thick. Press the cake into a firm layer using the back of the spoon. Spoon a layer of berries on top of the cake. Mix all liquors together. Pour enough liquor blend over the berries to coat and soak into the cake. Spoon a 1" layer of pudding on top of the berries, then a layer of whipped cream. Begin with another layer of cake, berries, liquor, etc. until the glasses are filled. Serve immediately or refrigerate overnight.

Serves: **6**

ALMOND COOKIE CAFE ALMOND COOKIES

The challenge with these cookies is to wait until they are cooked before eating them. The raw dough is so good, this will require a certain amount of discipline. Serve these cookies with hot tea as a pick-me-up in the afternoon or as the perfect light dessert, especially after one of the great Chinese meals in the chapter on main courses. These almond cookies were the only dessert on the menu at the Almond Cookie Cafe and there was never a single note in the suggestion box about offering anything else!

Ingredients:

1/3 cup honey
1/4 cup canola oil
2 tablespoons water
1 3/4 cup whole wheat flour
1 1/2 teaspoon almond extract
1 teaspoon baking soda
1/2 teaspoon cream of tartar
1/2 teaspoon sea salt
20 almonds, halved

Combine all ingredients except almonds and flour. Mix in half the flour at a time, stirring well. Drop onto a cookie sheet by the teaspoonful. Dip the palm of your hand in flour and flatten each cookie. Press almond half, white side up, into the center of each. Bake at 375 degrees for 6-8 minutes, or until lightly browned.

Makes: 35 cookies (if you haven't eaten any dough)

BERGAMOT BROWNIES

Flavor and beauty is added to these rich treats with the gorgeous flowers and heavenly scented leaves of the Bergamot mint plant. The flowers are bright red and make a great garnish and the leaves smell and taste of orange mint. These brownies are truly intended for only the most special of occasions since they are quite a splurge calorie-wise. Cut in small squares and this batch will go a long way.

Ingredients:

1 small package chocolate chips
6 tablespoons butter or margarine
2 eggs
1 teaspoon vanilla
1/3 cup honey
1/2 cup flour
1/2 teaspoon baking powder

Filling:

1-8 oz package cream cheese
1/3 cup honey
1 egg
1/4 teaspoon mint extract
12 Bergamot leaves and flowers (save flowers
   for garnish)

Melt chocolate chips and butter together. Beat thoroughly with 2 eggs, vanilla, honey, flour and baking powder. Pour half this mix into a 9x9 inch baking dish. Bake at 350 degreees for 10 minutes. Place all filling ingredients in the blender and blend until smooth. Spread evenly over cooked brownie mix, pour balance of uncooked brownie mix on top and bake for another 30 minutes. The filling and the uncooked brownie mix may swirl together a bit—don't worry—it makes the brownies that much prettier when sliced. Garnish each brownie with a single red flower. These brownies make great individual birthday cakes—add a candle to each one! Enjoy!

Serves: 12

GARDENS-BY-THE-BAY was established on the Central Coast of California in 1987 and has been producing the finest in herbal gourmet foods ever since.

PRODUCTS include: herbal vinegars, herbed oils, Southwestern specialties, soups, sauces, salad dressings, berry vinegars, herb charts and more!

For a catalogue, order form or list of retailers in your area, please write, call or FAX:

Gardens-by-the-Bay
Attn. Jackie Shaw
P.O. Box 1654
Morro Bay, California 93443

Phone/FAX: 805-462-1339

INDEX